# Ljubljana

## THE BRADT CITY GUIDE

**Robin & Jenny McKelvie**

Bradt Travel Guides Ltd, UK
The Globe Pequot Press Inc, USA

**First published April 2005**

Bradt Travel Guides Ltd
19 High Street, Chalfont St Peter, Bucks SL9 9QE, England; www.bradtguides.com
Published in the USA by The Globe Pequot Press Inc, 246 Goose Lane, PO Box 480,
Guilford, Connecticut 06437-0480



A catalogue record for this book is available from the British Library

ISBN-10: 1 84162 116 1
ISBN-13: 978 1 84162 116 6

*Front cover* Robin McKelvie (Ljubljanica River in spring) *Text photographs* Robin McKelvie
*Maps* Steve Munns *Illustrations* Carole Vincer

Typeset from the authors' disc by Wakewing
Printed and bound in Spain by Grafo SA, Bilbao

# Authors

**Robin McKelvie** has been a full-time travel writer and photographer since 1997 and is a member of both the British Guild of Travel Writers and the Outdoor Writers Guild. He has written about more than 50 European cities and travelled to 70 countries worldwide. He first visited Slovenia in 1992, and since then has covered the region, writing on Slovenia, Croatia and Montenegro. As well as guidebooks, his work has been published in over 40 magazines and newspapers around the world including the *Independent on Sunday, Independent Magazine, Sunday Herald, Scotsman, Scotland on Sunday, Guardian, Global Magazine, Wanderlust, CNN Traveller, Trailfinders, TNT, The Australian, Business Traveller, ABTA Travelspirit, Boom Magazine for Millionaires* and *International High Flyer.* Robin is also easyJet's 'Man in Ljubljana', writing destination reports on a monthly basis for their in-flight magazine in conjunction with his wife. Their *Slovenia: The Bradt Travel Guide* is due to be published in May 2005.

**Jenny McKelvie** has been working as a travel writer since 1998, a job that has taken her to destinations around the world and helped develop her specialist knowledge of central and eastern Europe. Her writing credits include *Highstyle, European Businessman, Classic Travel, People's Friend, Homes Away from Home, Alpha Traveller, TNT, Footloose* and *SX*. She also wrote the *Mintel Emerging Destination Report to Slovenia.* Jenny also helps write monthly updates on Ljubljana for easyJet's in-flight magazine.

# Contents

Contents

# Acknowledgements

Special thanks go to Petra Stušek at the Ljubljana Tourist Office for her unfaltering and invaluable help in the city she helped us love as much she does and to her predecessor Petra Čuk, now with Hoteli Bled, who offered her expert knowledge as well as unfaltering hospitality. Miro Gracin, formerly of the Slovenian Tourist Board, also aided with both practical help and incisive insights into the city and country, as did Mateja Tomin Vučkovič and Jona Senk, also of the STB. Our thanks also go out to Jan Orsič, who helped guide us around Ljubljana by boat and bike, Nina Turuk, Miha Kovacic, Janis Skok, Eva Ferjan, Matjaž Kos and Spela and Jaka Verbié Miklié. In the UK Angela Rennie at the Slovenian Tourist Board and Mary Stuart-Miller, the UK public relations contact, also deserve special thanks for their enthusiasm and assistance.

**DEDICATION**

To Rita and Peter, John and Gill –
as good parents as you could ever hope to have.

# Introduction

When I (Robin) told friends and family that I was planning to visit Ljubljana for the first time in 1992 the reactions, from those who had actually heard of the city, ranged from slight surprise, through to outright shock from others whose only experience of Slovenia was from TV news reports of the fighting that had erupted the year before during the break-up of Yugoslavia. The reality, though, was that even in 1992 Slovenia was completely safe to visit, as its only direct involvement in the regional conflicts had been a brief ten-day skirmish with the Yugoslav National Army (JNA) a year earlier as it quickly secured its independence.

Ljubljana has changed markedly over the last decade, but the things that first struck me – the remarkable collage of baroque and art-nouveau architecture, the sheer multitude of green space, the willow-strewn Ljubljanica River and citizens who actually live up to the 'friendly locals' clichés – still entrance today. On a crisp sunny morning as the distant Alpine mountains poke through and the whole city seems to be wandering by the café-kissed banks of the river, with the spires and elegant façades of the Old Town rising above, there are few other European cities I would rather be wandering in.

Since my first visit I have been back to Slovenia a dozen times, my wife usually accompanying me on each trip since we met in 1997, and it still amazes us that the tourist hordes have not yet descended on this unique hideaway that is sandwiched between Italy, Austria, Hungary and the Balkans. Although its epic sweep of scenery, everything from Alpine peaks and tumbling rivers in the north, to the balmy Adriatic coastline and vineyards in the south, are garnering increasing praise from the travel pages of magazines and newspapers, the country still remains genuinely 'unspoilt'. The same is true of the bijou capital, a neat and appealing city of under 270,000 inhabitants that manages to pack an incredible amount into a very compact and easily navigable space, but which rarely feels crowded or hectic.

All images of Balkan quagmires and political troubles dissolve as soon as you arrive in Ljubljana (pronounced 'Loobliana'). It is a place that is hard not to instantly fall in love with. If the well-preserved baroque architecture of the Old Town does not grab you then maybe it will be the lazy Ljubljanica as it meanders through the city's core, or the green lung of Tivoli Park with its outdoor sculpture and explosion of flowers. Perhaps you will be charmed by the pavement cafés and bountiful restaurants, where organic fresh produce and excellent Slovenian wine is the norm, or more cerebral attractions like the excellent Modern Art Gallery or National Gallery. Maybe it will just be something more subtle such as hearing the strains of a young student honing their violin skills from a flat right in the city centre, or how easy it is to strike up a conversation with its disarmingly friendly English-speaking citizens.

Whatever beguiles you in Ljubljana, few visitors can resist its charms and we were and are no exception. In short, we have fallen in love with almost everything about the city, a devotion that seems to grow with each arrival. Ljubljana is always changing as it looks and feels completely different with seasons worthy of the name. In summer you can dine al fresco, while when the leaves fall and the winter sweeps in the action moves indoors where warming mugs of mulled wine await. In spring the city slowly eases back to outdoor living as the last heavy snowfalls recede and the winter woollies are tucked away. Ljubljana in December feels like a completely different city from Ljubljana in August, a perfect excuse for repeat visits.

In just over a decade Slovenia has transformed itself from an unwilling appendage of Yugoslavia into a modern and successful European democracy. In 2004 Slovenia joined both NATO and the EU, something no other state in the old federation has yet managed. It is hard not to be impressed by Ljubljana and its hard-working, practical citizens, the *Ljubljančani*, for the way they have kept their heads down and fashioned their prosperous and upbeat capital.

Despite the country's move towards greater integration with Europe, Ljubljana still retains a real independent spirit that manifests itself in so many ways, some obvious but others more subtle. There is the outdoor market right in the heart of the city where, in a defiant stand against the world of supermarket hegemony, old ladies sell their homemade honey and farmers peddle vegetables plucked straight from their fields. It also comes out in the long, lazy lunches and languorous dinners that many people take, with a nonchalance that is far more Mediterranean than central European. The *Ljubljančani* themselves hate being labelled or categorised – they see themselves as citizens of the city, not eastern European nor central European and certainly not Balkan.

Today when we tell friends and family that we are planning to head back to

Ljubljana the reactions are very different from 1992. Now they often tell us that they want to come too as they know it came top of a travel poll in a newspaper or because they have heard of it eulogised as the 'new Prague'. Ljubljana is not the 'new Prague', nor the new anywhere else for that matter: it is simply one of Europe's most appealing escapes, a compact capital that we sincerely hope you will end up falling in love with as deeply as we have.

Robin and Jenny McKelvie

## *FEEDBACK REQUEST*

We visit Ljubljana many times each year and have been doing so since 1992, but as things change so fast we genuinely appreciate any feedback from readers. It helps us in putting together the next editions of the guidebook as well as other articles we write for magazines and newspapers. It is in all of our interests to keep things as up to date as possible. So if you love the city as much as we do, or if (perish the thought) you have somehow found something to hate about it, please do let us know, as every letter and email will be read and as many updates as possible included in the next edition. Warm regards, hvala.

All correspondence c/o Bradt Travel Guides, 19 High Street, Chalfont St Peter, Bucks SL9 9QE, England.

# How to Use this Book

**Symbols** Each map reference is followed by a code which indicates the location of venues listed in the book (see pages 25–30 for more information):

| | |
|---|---|
| OT | Old Town |
| C | Centre |
| OCC | Outside City Centre |
| KT | Krakovo & Trnovo |
| TK | Krajinski Park Tivoli |

**Map references** (eg: [1 B2]) relate to the colour map section at the end of the guide.

**Websites and email addresses** are published wherever possible. Where an establishment has a reliable website, we list the URL to allow readers to view photographs, current prices, menus and promotions etc.

**Hotel room rates** In the majority of listings these are given for single and double rooms. Where occupancy is available in triples, quads and suites prices for these are also given.

**Restaurant prices** include all taxes. It is customary to leave a tip of 10% unless the service has been really poor. The price range indicates options from a basic set menu to fine-dining à-la-carte options. You will find that the majority of restaurants post a copy of the menu in their windows, and many offer a set-price deal, particularly at lunch times, making it possible to find an affordable meal in some of the city's most expensive establishments. Prices quoted are intended as a guide only.

**Prices** quoted in the text were correct at the time of writing.

**Opening hours** Most bars and restaurants tend to open for lunch at around noon and stay open until 23.00 or 24.00 Monday to Saturday, some open an hour later on Sundays, while others open at 17.00 or are closed all day. Restaurants that open for breakfast generally welcome customers from 08.00 and also stay open through to 23.00 or 24.00. It is wise to make a reservation if you want to dine in Ljubljana's more expensive restaurants at night, particularly at weekends or in the summer. Closing times are often the only thing that really differentiates cafés from bars, with the majority of the cafés winding down before midnight, whilst bars generally stay open until 01.00. If you are a night owl there are plenty of late-opening bars that serve drinks until 02.00 or 03.00. Shopping hours are generally 09.00–19.00 Monday–Friday and 09.00–13.00 on Saturdays, with out-of-town malls open until 20.00 on Saturdays. Opening and closing times may vary by an hour or two. Banking hours are usua , Monday–Friday 08.30–12.30 and 14.00–17.00 (some open all day) and Saturday 08.30–12.00, while offices tend to open Monday–Friday 08.00–16.00.

**Credit cards** Most establishments accept payment by major credit card, including American Express, Diners Club, Mastercard/Eurocard and Visa. If in doubt you should check first.

## *LJUBLJANA AT A GLANCE*

**Location** Central Slovenia, 85km from Klagenfurt, 110km from Trieste, 135km from Zagreb and a two-hour direct flight from London
**Altitude** 298m above sea level
**Population** 265,881 (Government of the Republic of Slovenia, 2002)
**Language** Slovene
**Religion** Majority (67.9%) Roman Catholic (see *Religion*)
**Time zone** Central European GMT +1 hour
**International dialling code** +386
**Public holidays** January 1 and 2 (New Year), February 8 (Slovene Cultural Day), Easter Monday, April 27 (Resistance Day), May 1 and 2 (Labour Days), Pentecost, June 25 (Slovenia Day), August 15 (Feast of the Assumption), October 31 (Reformation Day), November 1 (All Saints' Day), December 25 (Christmas Day), December 26 (Independence Day)
**Climate** Average temperatures: winter –1°C, spring 10°C, summer 20°C and autumn 10°C
**Currency** Tolars (SIT): 1 tolar = 100 stotins
**Weights and measures** Metric system
**Electricity** 220V AC, frequency 50Hz, two-pin plugs with round prongs

boundaries are over a dozen churches, cultural Meccas like the National Gallery, City Museum and the Modern Art Gallery and a liberal sprinkling of other museums, with everything from the Museum of Beer Making through to the Railway Museum. Then there is the smorgasbord of small informal galleries that spring up and disappear as quickly, all part of the thriving cultural scene.

Ljubljana was always a cultural hub in the former Yugoslavia with an aggressively avant-garde reputation and this vivacity still ripples through the city today with an artistically literate population and a large and active student community. One-off cultural performances and various 'happenings' are all the rage and you are as likely to hear one of the sunglasses-and-mobile-phone-sporting local students talking through the latest experimental theatre as you are their favourite cutting-edge DJs.

Ljubljana has one of the youngest populations of any European capital and the city centre is awash with strutting young *Ljubljančani* decked out in the latest designer fashions. This youthfulness comes through strongly in the city's vibrant nightlife, which buzzes with a plethora of bright new-style bars, hip cafés and quality restaurants. Venues seem to open and close with alarming regularity in Ljubljana as fickle patrons look for the next 'in' place to see and be seen, which helps keeps things fresh.

One of the few downsides to life in the Slovenian capital is the weather. There is no hiding the fact that this is one of the wettest capital cities in Europe and that the chilly, snow-ridden winters can linger on into April. The *Ljubljančani*, though, are well used to their climatic extremes and make the most of them, and visitors are well advised to follow suit. If it is snowing wrap up and enjoy the castle bathed in a white cloak, or if it rains duck inside for a warming *bela kava* or pop into one of the numerous museums. When the sun re-emerges over the Ljubljanica it makes it all the more special as you have endured the climatic ravages like a true citizen of the city.

Whatever the climatic extremes everything seems to work in Ljubljana. While London is brought to its knees by the slightest snowfall and Paris collapses from humidity Ljubljana seems to just stride on. Citizens from other more 'Westernised' cities are often heard enviously remarking on this clean, efficient city with its gleaming new buses, tireless street cleaners and prosperous ambience. Some locals like to joke that it is simply because they have a female mayor, Danica Simšic.

When Slovenia joined the EU in 2004 the event was greeted with muted celebrations, rather than the scenes of wild joy witnessed in some corners of the new Europe. Slovenia and Ljubljana have been doing very nicely thank you since 1991 and some locals fear that the coming of EU hegemony and a whirl of directives could be a bad thing for the capital. They may not need to worry too much, as this is a city that has always kept its unique and vivacious identity intact no matter who holds sway over the country, whether it be the Austro–Hungarians or the Yugoslav Socialists. Soon other increasingly multi-national and faceless European cities could be casting an envious eye to this independent slice of city living. Perhaps it may not be long before other cities are promoting themselves as the 'new Ljubljana'.

The future for the Slovenian capital looks as bright as a crisp winter's day by the Ljubljanica. Its strategic location, with easy access through a rapidly improving

## *JOŽE PLEČNIK*

The seminal Slovene architect Jože Plečnik is to Ljubljana what Haussmann was to Paris. He had an even greater influence on his city as his touch is almost everywhere. Born in 1872, Plečnik had a grand vision for Ljubljana, which he wanted to be the Slovenian Athens, a spiritual home for a people who were in the process of discovering and developing their national identity. He honed his considerable talents in Graz and at the Vienna Academy of Fine Arts, later lecturing at the Prague Academy and working right up to his death in 1957. A modest and religious man, he took on a multitude of projects, many of them on an epic scale and dared to use unfashionable materials like concrete, often out of economic necessity, but still managed to infuse all his work with a quiet dignity and human dimension. For those with plenty of time in the city a day spent exploring his legacy is fascinating. There is his landmark Triple Bridge, the nearby Cobbler's Bridge, his remodelling of the banks of the Ljubljanica, the Križanke theatre complex, his bridge in Trnovo and, of course, the National and University Library, which many *Ljubljančani* rate as Plečnik's masterpiece. Then there is his work adding the colonnades to the Central Market, the entrance to the Žale Cemetery and in Tivoli Park; the list as extensive as it is impressive in its unfaltering quality.

network of motorways to Austria, Italy, Hungary and Croatia, as well as Slovenia's own Adriatic seafront, give it an importance and potential far above its size. Many metropoles have been pushed as the 'gateway to the east' and Ljubljana is indeed ideally situated for dealing with the new ex-communist EU members. It is also, perhaps even more crucially, an EU member with direct access to the untapped economies of the Balkan region, one of the least-developed corners of Europe, which has only now settled down after the decade of wars that Slovenia so cleverly managed to extricate itself from. With tourists finally starting to visit this criminally undiscovered gem and a bountiful future as an economic hub on the horizon few should, as many *Ljubljančani* are fond of saying, 'bet against the small guy'.

## HISTORY

According to local legend, Ljubljana's first inhabitants came straight from the pages of Greek mythology, when, after being tricked into stealing a golden fleece that belonged to King Aeetes, Jason and his Argonauts fled from Colchis. The *Argo* then transported the ancient warriors on their epic adventure from the Black Sea to the Danube, onward to the Sava River and finally into the Ljubljanica. Having successfully escaped the wrath of Aeetes, Jason and the Argonauts were confronted by a formidable fire-breathing dragon, which, during a fierce battle, the brave hero managed to slay. In commemoration of this courageous act the city's coat of arms still bears the picture of the beast. The Ljubljana dragon can also be found throughout the city, on the castle's tower, the town hall and railings along the banks of the Ljubljanica, as well as standing proud on the eponymous bridge and, of course, on a wealth of tourist souvenirs.

While it may not be full of colourful characters from Greek mythology, Ljubljana's recorded history is no less intoxicating. You should always, though, take any recent stab at Slovenian history with a pinch of salt as over the last decade the country has been free for the first time to really explore, and some critics would suggest rewrite, its history and heritage. It is wise, though, not to challenge the highly subjective version of history you hear from an animated local in this part of the world.

Situated at the heart of Europe on a crossroads between east and west, and providing central Europe's access to the Mediterranean Sea through the Adriatic, Slovenia has long attracted a diverse range of settlers and invaders. Historical evidence suggests that Ljubljana's first inhabitants were pile dwellers from the Copper Age, who lived in stilt-houses built on marshland. Next came the Illyrians, who settled near Ljubljana in the late Bronze Age. Cave paintings near the capital depict members of this ancient tribe engaged in battle and sporting events, enjoying great feasts and conducting ritual sacrifices. Around the 3rd century BC Celtic tribes rumbled into the region.

## The Romans and Slavs

The arrival of the Romans in the 1st century BC saw Ljubljana's status elevated from a rough tribal settlement to a military base and later to a city. Under the Romans Ljubljana became Emona and remnants of the Roman settlement can still be found on the left bank of the Ljubljanica, including reconstructed sections of the Roman walls. For its residents life in Emona was good save the frequent attacks by the barbarian Huns and the Central Asian Avars, but the Romans finally capitulated in AD452.

Historians dispute the timescale of the arrival of the first Slavic settlers in Slovenia; some sources reckon that Slavs from the west migrated here as early as AD500. What is certain is that by the 7th century the Slavs had become the dominant people in Slovenia, establishing the first independent Slavic or Slovenian state, Carinthia. In AD746 Carinthia fell under the auspices of the Bavarian Dukes.

## The medieval period

Ljubljana next emerged as a significant city in medieval times, with its Austrian name Laibach (a name that it kept until 1918) first appearing in written documents in 1144. In 1335, under the Austro–Hungarians, Ljubljana became the capital of the province of Carniola, and the Austro–Hungarians remained the dominant force in the city until the end of World War I.

During their 600-reign the Austro–Hungarians confronted many challenges, including repeat invasion attempts by the Turks in the middle of the 15th century and a devastating earthquake in 1511 that felled much of Ljubljana.

While reconstruction after the earthquake helped shape the city's physical appearance, Protestantism, which rose to the fore in the late 16th century, played a significant role in shaping the city's psyche over the next 200 years. One of the most significant events during this time was the 1550 publication of the first book written entirely in the Slovene language – Primož Trubar's *Catechismus in Abecedarium*.

## Cultural and political influences

Other influential figures, who, like Trubar, resided in Ljubljana and campaigned for the cultural and political freedoms of the Slovene people, include the satirical writer Ivan Cankar and the Romantic poet France Prešeren. All three men remain writ large on the national conscious of modern Slovenia and, more than 150 years after his death in 1849, a looming statue of Prešeren still watches protectively over Ljubljana's residents. Protestantism also witnessed the establishment of a number of significant cultural institutions, including a scientific academy, an academy for fine arts and a philharmonic society. Towards the end of the 18th century the latter was held in such high esteem that world-famous composers like Beethoven, Brahms, Paganini and Haydn were amongst its honorary members.

## The Austro–Hungarians

At the beginning of the 19th century Napoleon made a brief incursion into the region, which left Ljubljana as the capital of the French emperor's Illyrian Provinces from 1809 to 1813. During this period the Slovene language was allowed to openly flourish as was the distinctive national identity that had been suppressed by the Austro–Hungarians. Napoleon's downfall saw the redrawing of the map of Europe and the return of Slovenia to Austro–Hungarian rule at the 1814 Congress of Vienna. It was here that the Habsburg Prince Klemens von Metternich agreed to join the Holy Alliance, swearing to uphold the principles of authoritarian rule and Christianity.

With Austro–Hungarian rule restored, the other defining events in Ljubljana's history were the construction of the Vienna–Trieste railway, which was completed in 1857 and brought new cultural influences to the Slovenian capital (though to some extent the railway's strategic and economic importance was dampened by the opening of a Vienna–Trieste route four years later) and a second devastating earthquake in 1895. The rebuilding of the city in the late 19th and early 20th century gave rise to the stunning art-nouveau (or secessionist) buildings found in Ljubljana's historic left bank.

## World War I and II

World War I heralded the end of four decades of peace in Europe and the collapse of the Austro–Hungarian Empire. In 1918 Slovenia became part of the Kingdom of Serbs, Croats and Slovenes. The inter-war years saw the city take on much of its iconic architecture, under the guiding hand of Jože Plečnik, Ljubljana's seminal architect. At this time the biggest skyscraper in Yugoslavia, the Nebotičnik, was constructed. Currently closed due to a legal wrangle brought on by the process of denationalisation, the skyscraper still stands on Slovenska Street as an enduring testimony to the grand ambitions of the newly independent pan-Slavic country.

In 1939 war engulfed Europe once again. After staying on the sidelines for over a year the kingdom entered the fray and was soon swallowed up by the Axis powers, with Germany, Italy and Hungary dividing Slovenia between them. This dark period in Slovenia's history was clouded by massacres, the suppression of Slovenian identity, the collaboration of the Slovenian Home Guard and the murder of thousands of the latter by the partisans in the denouement of the war, an event that only came to light in the 1970s.

A dramatically different Slovenia emerged from the rubble of World War II, and in 1945 Ljubljana took its place as one of the six capitals of Tito's new Yugoslavia. The federation's other capitals were Belgrade in Serbia, Zagreb in Croatia, Sarajevo in Bosnia-Herzegovina, Skopje in Macedonia and Titograd (Podgorica) in Montenegro. For almost half a century the Slovenian capital found itself under the rigid control of a socialist regime, characterised by dictatorial leadership and the shared ownership of property. Slovenia was the most prosperous per capita part of the federation, but under the socialist system the wealth was redistributed to less-developed regions such as Serbia and Montenegro, a siphoning of resources that was to turn many Slovenes against the idea of Yugoslavia. This animosity grew amidst recurrent stories of government corruption, nepotism and attempts to suppress Slovenian identity.

## Slovenian independence

On December 23 1990, an overwhelming majority of voters asserted their desire to leave the Socialist Federal Republic of Yugoslavia and become an independent country. After a delay of six months independence was officially declared on June

26 1991, a move that led to a ten-day war with Yugoslav government troops. Mercifully this brief conflict was relatively bloodless. Over 2,000 soldiers from the Yugoslav National Army (JNA) were ordered to seize the country's border stations, however blockades prevented the majority from leaving their barracks and the well-organised Slovenian domestic forces proved themselves a match for the confused and demoralised JNA troops, some of whom were actually Slovene. After ten days of skirmishes and threats to attack Brnik Airport and Ljubljana itself – a menace that never materialised – the JNA backed down and a cease-fire took effect on July 6 1991. The only evidence in Ljubljana of the war were false air-raid alarms and the Yugoslav army helicopter that was shot down over Rožna Dolina near Tivoli Park.

Slovenia's independence was recognised by the EU on January 15 1992, followed by the USA on April 17 1992. The country then set about developing its economy and building political and economic relationships with the rest of the world. Slovenia's integration into the European fold was complete in 2004 when it joined both the EU and NATO. Potential political problems do remain such as the lingering dispute with Croatia over territorial waters in the Adriatic, but for the fledgling nation of Slovenia and its capital the future looks bright.

## POLITICS

The political history of modern-day Slovenia is a relatively short one, which begins with their assertion of independence in 1991 (see *History*). One of the biggest tasks that confronted the newly independent country was the implementation of a new constitution, which materialised in December 1991, under the guidance of the country's first democratically elected prime minister, Lojze Peterle. This new constitution established a democratic parliamentary political system, which clearly delineated the roles of separate judicial, legislative and executive powers. Under this model of government the National Assembly (*Državni Zbor*), which has the final say in legislative issues, is the most powerful institution. Slovenia's National Council (*Državni Svet*) – which represents the interests of the city and its workforce – has the power to challenge legislation passed by the National Assembly and can also initiate legislative change.

In principle the referendums held by the National Assembly create a transparent political process that directly involves the people. Recent referendums include ballots on membership of the EU and NATO in March 2003, as well as one on weekend opening hours for retail outlets. Some Slovenes now feel many of these numerous referendums are a waste of money and that state funds could be used more prudently. Others cast aspersions on the authenticity of this process, claiming that the majority of Slovenes did not want to join NATO and yet the result was overwhelmingly in favour of this.

Slovenia's judicial system comprises four different types of court – district, regional, higher and supreme – with the latter being the most powerful. District Court judges deal with lesser offences, while those in Regional Courts deal with minors, business law and land registration. Higher Court judges are responsible for repeat offenders and appeals made against the rulings of District and Regional Courts. The principal role of the Supreme Court is that of reviewing appeals, settling disputes over jurisdiction and regulating the legal profession.

Slovenia's government holds executive powers, and the country's current government is led by Prime Minister Janez Janša, leader of the Slovenian Democratic Party (SDS), who took up his post in December 2004, two months after the October elections. The other three parties of the government are New Slovenia Party (NSi), the Slovenian People's Party (SLS) and the Pensioners' Party (DeSUS). In addition to the prime minister the government has 14 cabinet members. Slovenia's other political parties include the Liberal Democratic Party (LDS), the United List of Social Democrats (ZLSDS), the Slovene National Party (SNS), the Slovenian Youth Party (SMS) and the Greens of Slovenia.

Dr Janez Drnovšek, Slovenia's second prime minister, is now the country's president. Elected as the Head of State with 56% of the vote in December 2002, Drnovšek resigned his post as prime minister the following day. According to the Slovenian Constitution the president is the country's commander in chief and is restricted to a maximum of ten years in office (two five-year terms). Presidential duties include calling elections, nominating a candidate for prime minister and appointing ambassadors and other state officials. Although Drnovšek has held a prominent political office since 1992, it has not always been plain sailing for him. In May 2000 a vote of no confidence forced him to leave his post, and Dr Andrej Bajuk of the New Slovenian Party (with centre-right leanings) took over. Six months later parliamentary elections returned the LDS to power and Drnovšek to his post as prime minister.

In recent years the political stage in Slovenia has been dominated by the rapid privatisation of business and preparation for EU membership, which this young country achieved with impressive speed and efficiency on May 1 2004, giving Slovenia access to an internal trade market of 455 million people. Since 1991 Slovenia has also joined the United Nations, the Council of Europe and NATO, as well as becoming a non-permanent member of the United Nations Security Council.

## ECONOMY

Slovenia has a strong and growing economy, which is set to go from strength to strength as a result of the country's accession to the EU in May 2004. Far from being an impoverished new member, Slovenia's GNP actually rose above that of more-established EU members Portugal and Greece in 2004. The country's GDP has witnessed a steady annual growth since 1991 and inflation has been falling in recent years – this stood at 9.1% in 1991 and just 5.5% in 2003. The number of unemployed people in Slovenia has also been declining since the late 1990s, and the country had an unemployment rate of 6.3% in December 2003. On a national level agriculture, fishing, education, health, construction, manufacturing and service industries are the biggest employers. In Ljubljana itself the pharmaceutical, petrochemical and food-processing companies are the biggest contributors to the city's economy. Retail, financial and business services, public services, tourism, catering and construction are also important employers in the capital. Ljubljana generates around 25% of Slovenia's GDP. The only clouds on the economic horizon are the structural economic legacies of socialism (such as the power of the strong trade unions) and the rising domestic costs that have already led some international companies to seek new, more cost-effective bases elsewhere in the expanded EU.

## PEOPLE

The *Ljubljančani* are generally warm and welcoming, extending a genuine hand of friendship and talking about themselves modestly, often underselling the beauty of their city. Yet the same people are also sometimes capable of expressing surprisingly direct opinions that can occasionally come across as arrogant or downright rude. Part of this bluntness comes from a desire to be honest, so don't ask a local how you look unless you are prepared to hear that the cut of your jacket doesn't suit you or that you need a haircut. With such an ethnically homogenous nation views towards others of different nationalities and races, particularly Croats and Montenegrins, can also sometimes veer towards prejudice.

One of the first things that strikes visitors to Ljubljana is the youthfulness of its population, with the city's 58,000 students accounting for over 20% of the residents. Ljubljana's young inhabitants contribute to the city's casual, laid-back atmosphere and a sense of romance. Inspired by their famous forefathers Trubar, Cankar and Prešeren many of the city's aspiring young poets put pen to paper in what has been lovingly described as a 'national affliction'. This is a country, after all, where they have a national holiday dedicated to culture.

To sum up, the residents of Ljubljana are as a whole vivacious, friendly and direct people, who have a love of literature, art and outdoor life. Although they may not always be tactful, the *Ljubljančani* are unfailingly generous and hospitable. When we were invited to a new friend's house for the first time she spoiled us with a three-course meal, champagne and lashings of wine, and even arranged for a lift to her home. Yet some expatriates who live in the city claim that they have never been invited into the house of a local, so if you do get an invitation ensure you make the most of it.

## RELIGION

A public opinion survey conducted in 2003 revealed that the majority of Slovenes, 67.9% of the population, are Roman Catholics, however many do not strictly adhere to the principles of their faith. The next biggest religion in Slovenia is the Serb Orthodox faith (2.3%), followed by Islam (1.2%), other Christians (0.9%) and Evangelists (0.7%). In this same survey 23.1% of respondents reported that they were agnostic. Despite the relative homogeneity in the population, there are a further 30 registered religious societies in Slovenia. Given the divisions, hatred and violence that religion has become synonymous within the Balkans, Slovenes as a rule are pretty tolerant when it comes to religion, though seriously bad publicity was generated for the country thanks to a recent bid to block the construction of Ljubljana's first mosque.

## CULTURE AND FESTIVALS

Ljubljana is a city rich in culture, which boasts numerous museums, galleries and theatres, including the Slovene National Theatre and the Slovene National Opera and Ballet Theatre. Ljubljana is also home to one of the world's oldest philharmonic orchestras, a thriving club scene, an abundance of music venues and art-house cinemas. Each year Ljubljana plays host to a variety of international events, the highlight of which is the Ljubljana Summer Festival.

### January

**New Year's Concert** Welcome in the New Year with the Slovenian Philharmonic Orchestra (www.filharmonija.si).

### *FRANCE PREŠEREN*

No-one more vividly and emotively captures the tragic and romantic emotions of the *Ljubljančani* than Slovenian poet France Prešeren. It is fitting that Prešeren's verse is used today as the national anthem ('A Toast') and that it is his figure that stands grandly overlooking the square dedicated to him in central Ljubljana. Prešeren was born in 1800 in a village near the capital, with the most romantic and tragic phase of his life initiated at a service in the Church of St John the Baptist in Trnovo where he fell madly in love with the teenage Julija

## February

**The Tercets of Trnovo** Three-day festival of poetry held at the KUD France Prešeren Cultural Centre.

## March

**Women's Day Social Gathering** Seize the chance to meet local women at this free event held in the International Centre of Graphic Arts.

## April

**Slovenian Musical Days** This event is organised by Festival Ljubljana and showcases contemporary music by Slovenian and European composers.

Primic. She was from a wealthy family and her parents were less than impressed with the poet lawyer's prospects and the two were destined never to be together. A lonely and heartbroken Prešeren died prematurely in 1849 in Kranj, and much of his best verse was inspired by his feelings for Primic. Many visitors mistake the semi-naked muse (the subject of much controversy when it was revealed in 1905) above his figure in Prešernov trg to be Julija, but she is actually depicted in a bust on the front of a building on adjacent Wolfova, with some locals rather unkindly suggesting she is there to eternally mock him.

## May

**Exodos** (www.exodos-festival.si) An annual festival of contemporary performing arts, with past performances by Japanese drummers and Vietnamese puppeteers. The main venue for shows is the Cankarjev Dom.

## June

**Druga Godba** (www.drugagodba.si) The outdoor Križanke theatre is the main venue for five days of alternative and eclectic concerts by international performers. Founded in 1985 and a local favourite, Druga Godba literally means 'alternative bands', with the diverse music on offer ranging from modern jazz and ethno-electronic to folk music and African beats.

**Summer Night of Museums** An open-door event that gives access to museums, exhibitions and galleries in Ljubljana. Free workshops, tours, concerts, film screenings, performances, lectures and presentations also take place on this day.

**Summer in Ljubljana Old Town** A series of free concerts staged in the Old Town's streets, squares, churches and courtyards (June–August).

**Ana Desetnica International Street Theatre Festival** (www.anadesetnica.org) One of Europe's largest street-theatre festivals.

## July–September

**Ljubljana Jazz Festival** This three-day event has been running for almost half a century and has performances by Slovene and international musicians.

**Trnfest** A five-day celebration of alternative culture including video, dance, music, theatre, exhibitions and events for children.

**Ljubljana Summer Festival** During the capital's biggest festival Ljubljana stages fill with performers from around the world and an additional 50,000 visitors flock to the city. Musical, theatrical and dance performances take place in the Slovenian Philharmonic Hall, Cankarjev Dom, Križanke summer theatre, Ljubljana Castle and the Cultural and Congress Centre (July and August).

**Mini Summer Festival** This children's festival with its puppet shows and children's theatre is a perfect complement to the Ljubljana Summer Festival (July–September).

## October

**Ljubljana Marathon** (www.marathon.slo-timing.com) An annual sporting event catering to all level of athletes, with a full marathon, half-marathon and fun run .

**Medieval Day** Reviving life in the Slovene capital during the Middle Ages, with Ljubljana Castle as a spectacular venue.

**City of Women** (www.cityofwomen-a.si) Celebrating the artistic talents and achievements of women.

## November

**Ljubljana International Wine Festival** A chance to taste more than 300 wines including those produced in Slovenia.

**Ljubljana International Film Festival** (www.ljubljanafilmfestival.org) More than 100 films from around the world including South Korea and Japan are screened at the Cankarjev Dom, Slovenska Kinoteka and other venues throughout the city.

**Ljubljana Gay and Lesbian Film Festival** November and December.

## December

**Festive December** A series of Christmas and New Year concerts.

**December in Ljubljana** Seasonal festivities throughout the city.

**Christmas and New Year Fair** Seasonal gifts and food (December and January).

**New Year's Eve** Join in the revelry on Kongresni trg and watch the fireworks as they explode over Ljubljana Castle at midnight.

The Ljubljana Tourist Board print free annual, monthly and weekly event guides. This information is also available on their website (www.ljubljana-tourism.si).

## GEOGRAPHY

The Republic of Slovenia is one of Europe's smallest countries. For comparison, it is around the same size as Wales or half the size of Switzerland. Located in central Europe, Slovenia shares borders with Croatia, Italy, Austria and Hungary. Ljubljana is at the heart of the country and is within an easy three-hour drive of even the most distant parts of the country. This compact size means that the country's dramatic mountains, thousands of underground caves, forests, Adriatic coast, lakes and rivers are all within easy reach of Ljubljana. The Ljubljanica River neatly divides the capital, with the city centre on the left bank and the Old Town on the right bank. Outside the city centre, the Gradaščica Canal separates the suburbs of Krakovo and Trnovo, while to the west is the Krajinski Park Tivoli (the Landscape Park of Tivoli).

## CLIMATE

Ljubljana has a continental climate with mild, often hot, summers, and cold winters. July and August are the warmest months in Ljubljana, with an average temperature of 20°C and highs hovering around 25°C. Days in May, June and September are also often pleasantly warm with average temperatures of 14–17°C, and maximums that can exceed 20°C. April and October, which traditionally mark the beginning and end of the tourist season in Ljubljana are slightly colder with average temperatures of 10°C and highs of 15°C. December, January and February are the coldest months in the city, with an average temperature of –1°C. In January and February the mercury can plummet as low as –5°C and rarely rises above 2°C. On the upside, December to March are the driest months in Ljubljana. There is no getting away from the fact that Ljubljana is one of the wettest capital cities in Europe and most locals make sure their umbrellas are never too far away.

# Planning

## LJUBLJANA – A PRACTICAL OVERVIEW

Ljubljana has come a long way since its first citizens scrambled together stilt-houses on the exposed marshland. The Romans built the first real city, an important hub on the trading and military artery that cut through the Alps from Italy to the central European plains. While Ljubljana has never been razed by man nature has made more than one stab at wiping it off the map with a series of earthquakes and floods. The powerful quake of 1895 in some ways today can be seen as a blessing as it allowed Jože Plečnik to try to conjure up the Slovenian Athens he had always dreamed of. His hand is everywhere and coupled with a colourful collage of baroque, art nouveau and Italianate architectural styles this small city manages to pack in a remarkable amount of diversity.

Forming a natural divide through Ljubljana is the Ljubljanica River, a sleepy stretch of pea-green water kissed by drooping willows. On the right bank is the rambling baroque Old Town and the lofty crag of Ljubljana Castle, while across the three landmark bridges (Triple Bridge, Dragon's Bridge and Cobbler's Bridge) is the pancake-flat left bank, the real hub of city life with the commercial centre and most of the hotels and cultural attractions, as well as the green expanse of the Tivoli and Krajinski parks. Ljubljana is the perfect size to negotiate on foot or by bike – cycling is something of a national obsession – but there is also a cheap, efficient and comprehensive public bus service on hand if legs become weary. The parts of the

### *WHEN IS A SQUARE NOT A SQUARE?*

The Slovene word for a 'square' is trg, but it is far more flexible shape-wise than its English-language counterpart. In the Old Town most of the squares are really long streets, but just to confuse things Prešernov trg, the city's most famous square, on the right bank, is just about square. Nearby Kongresni trg is neatly rectangular while also on the left bank Trg Francoske Revolucije is little more than a statue of Napoleon and a traffic junction.

city of most interest can be divided into four main zones, with the first two – the Old Town and Centre – the most crucial. The southern suburbs of Krakovo and Trnovo are also well worth exploring, while the parks of Tivoli and Krajinski offer a green escape. For an idea of the layout of the city look out for the bronze relief of Ljubljana that was placed on the corner of Prešernov trg and Čopova as Slovenia gained its independence in 1991.

## Old Town [OT]

The Old Town centres on three 'squares' – Mestni (town), Stari (old) and Gornji (upper). Starting by Robba's fountain, just across the Triple Bridge, the three squares rumble south in a flourish of cobbles with enticing baroque (and the odd medieval) buildings crowding above. This is the most charming part of the city to wander around and, despite a few tourist shops, it is still very much full of real life with boutique outlets, cafés and informal restaurants, not to mention residents who have the pleasure of living in one of the most appealing Old Towns in Europe. Running parallel to the squares just a block to the west is the riverside Cankarjevo nabrežje with its pavement cafés and sprinkling of niche clothing and jewellery stores.

Gornji trg takes a turn to the southeast and starts to climb up the hill that is home to Ljubljana Castle. Another way to get up this incline is from the cathedral, which lies to the north of Mestni trg. The cathedral and the Central Market, with its grand Plečnik-designed colonnades, lie overlooking the river and behind them Študentovska leads up a narrow twist through woodland to the castle. However you reach the castle it offers the same sweeping views out over the capital and on towards the Kamniške Savinje Alps to the north and the mountains of Gorenjska to the northwest.

## Centre [C]

The hub of the left bank Centre is Prešernov trg, the busiest square in the city. The square is surrounded by a flourish of interesting buildings, including the Franciscan Church of the Annunciation, the Hauptman House, the Centromerkur store and the Triple Bridge, which leads from here right across the Ljubljanica to the Old Town. Centre is blessed with some of Europe's finest secessionist architecture, on a par with Riga or anywhere in Germany. Follow Miklošičeva north, past the landmark Grand Union Hotel, and you are embraced by a collage of art nouveau façades.

To the south of Prešernov trg is a willow-strewn riverside walkway, Hribarjevo nabrežje, which soon becomes Breg and mirrors the right bank with its pavement cafés and restaurants. Running parallel to Breg to the west is Vegova, the heart of the university quarter with Plečnik's remarkable National and University Library.

To the west of the river, accessible by stairs from Hribarjevo nabrežje is Kongresni trg, another important public space, which sadly only really comes alive during big events. From Kongresni trg a tunnel leads through to Trg Republike, the grand legacy of socialist-era city planning with its mass of concrete and intimidating architecture. Cut northwest from Kongresni trg and you are firmly in the cultural quarter with the National Gallery, Modern Art Gallery and Opera House all in close proximity.

## Krajinski Park Tivoli [TK]

From the Modern Art Gallery a tunnel leads under the railway track west into Ljubljana's green lung. When you tell most *Ljubljančani* that they have one of Europe's finest city parks they usually look confused, before shrugging 'oh, Tivoli'. With so much bucolic splendour spread all over the country the *Ljubljančani* tend to underrate this oasis right on the edge of the city centre.

For anyone from one of Europe's more 'urban' cities Tivoli is close to paradise. Tivoli was built to mimic an English-style garden with well laid-out walkways, symmetrically planted trees and manicured flowerbeds. In the park's northwestern corner is the Modern History Museum and the Tivoli Hall complex, while behind is a wilder and more overgrown escape with rough paths and jogging trails.

Strolling around here, surrounded by vaulting trees on all sides, the city feels very far away indeed.

## Krakovo and Trnovo [KT]

South of Centre, and easily accessible from Breg along the river, is Krakovo. This sleepy suburb feels more like a Gorenjska village than a suburb with grand old houses and large vegetable gardens. This is where some of the smaller-scale stalls

### WHAT TO SEE AND DO

#### *If you are staying for a weekend*

- Savour the baroque Old Town
- Enjoy a *bela kava* or a glass of Union by the banks of the Ljubljanica
- Join Prešeren in his eponymous square and soak up the architecture
- Take a free bike for a spin around the pancake-flat left bank
- Explore the lively Central Market or, on Sundays, the flea market
- Hike up to Ljubljana Castle
- Indulge in a romantic evening boat cruise on the Ljubljanica
- Settle into an outdoor seat at Café Maček at night and watch the action
- Catch some culture – take in a play, concert, film or the opera
- Miss your flight and stay on in Ljubljana – you know you want to

in the Central Market source their wares. Strolling along Krakovska you will uncover a very different Ljubljana, where it feels like the 20th century, let alone the 21st century, is yet to arrive.

While Krakovo has few real sights, the same cannot be said of neighbouring Trnovo further to the south across the Gradaščica (often referred to as the Trnovo Canal). Here you will find the church where Prešeren first met his beloved Julija Primic and behind it the house where Plečnik lived for 40 years, now a museum.

### *If you are staying longer*

- Take time to explore the contrasting National and Modern Art galleries
- Join a guided walking or cycling tour
- Delve into the twin suburbs of Krakovo and Trnovo
- Explore Tivoli Park
- Go on a trawl of the city's array of fascinating churches
- Learn some Slovene, a devilishly hard language, but worth it for the positive reactions it will garner
- Try out a selection of the city's excellent and criminally good-value restaurants
- Head out of the city and climb Šmarna Gora
- Get out and explore Slovenia – one of Europe's great travel 'secrets'
- Get a job, buy a house and enjoy life in one of Europe's most liveable capitals

Follow the banks of the Gradaščica and you will come across what is claimed to be the only bridge in Europe with trees growing on it, another Plečnik creation.

Anything outside of these areas we refer to as **OCC** (Outside City Centre).

## WHEN TO VISIT (AND WHY)

There really is no bad time to visit Ljubljana. In summer it offers al-fresco living with many of its cafés, bars and restaurants exploding on to the streets in a flurry of tables. This is the season when the *Ljubljančani* strut their way around town in their finest designer gear, seeing and being seen, and it can be a thrilling time to be in the city. However, at weekends throughout the summer many locals flee to their coastal or mountain retreats.

In autumn when the city's bountiful trees start to change colour and shed their leaves Ljubljana is an incredibly romantic place to be as you kick your way through the leaves by the river. Many of the pavement cafés keep their tables out giving you the best of the summer without the humidity of July and August. September vies with May for being the best month to visit, as the chill of winter still seems a long way off.

Winter is the season that tends to put off many would-be visitors, worried that they will be frozen by the ravages of a continental European winter. True, the mercury can plummet, but the weather can also be glorious with clear blue skies accompanying walks across the crisp, fresh snow. If you follow the locals and wrap up warm and pepper your visit with plenty of glasses of the warming mulled wine, then winter can be a great time to visit, especially around Christmas, when there is a seasonal market, and New Year, when the city is engulfed by a giant street party.

Come spring, the snows start to ease and the city hauls itself back into life. The café tables, gingerly at first, ease their way back out on to the pavements and warmly clad *Ljubljančani* eagerly enjoy their first al-fresco *bela kava* of the year. With greenery returning all around and a real sense of rebirth this is one of the most enjoyable seasons, with May the pick of the spring months as any lingering snowfall finally dissipates and flickers of summer sun and warmth tease into the city.

Ljubljana's lively cultural and artistic scene also ensures that there is plenty to do all year round with a string of events and festivals (see *Culture and festivals*).

## TOUR OPERATORS

The Slovenian Tourist Board can provide a full list of tour operators based in your country of residence. Contact details for your closest office can be found at www.slovenia-tourism.si.

### UK and Ireland

Major companies offering city breaks in Ljubljana and organising tours to other parts of Slovenia include:

**Balkan Holidays** Sofia House, 19 Conduit St, London W1S 2BH; tel: +44 0845 130 1114; email: res@balkanholidays.co.uk; www.balkanholidays.co.uk

**Just Slovenia** The Barns, Woodlands End, Mells, Frome, Somerset BA11 3A; tel: +44 01373 814230; fax: +44 01373 813444; email: justslovenia@planos.co.uk; www.justslovenia.co.uk

**Kompas London Ltd** 2 Canfield Pl, London NW6 3BT; tel: +44 020 7372 3844; fax: +44 020 7372 3763; email: kompas.london@virgin.net; www.kompas.net

**Major Travel** Fortess Grove, London NW5 2HB; tel: +44 0870 330 7315; email: sales@majortravel.co.uk; www.majortravel.co.uk

**Regent Holidays** 15 John St, Bristol BS1 2HR; tel: +44 0117 921 1711; fax: +44 0117 925 4866; email: regent@regent-holidays.co.uk; www.regent-holidays.co.uk

**Vamos Travel** Fernwood House, Brindley Brae, Kinver, West Midlands DY7 6LR; tel: +44 01384 878125; fax: +44 0870 7621016; email: info@vamostravel.com; www.vamostravel.com

## USA

**Kompas Holidays International** 2929 E Commercial Bd, Suite 201, Ft Lauderdale, Florida 33308; tel: +1 954 771 9200 or 1 800 233 6422 (from within USA); fax: +1 954 771 9841; email: kompas@kompas.net; www.kompas.net

## Canada

**Kompas Tours International** PO Box 474 'Westmount Station', Montreal, Quebec, Canada H3Z 2T6; tel: +1 514 938 4041; fax: +1 514 938 4039; email: kompas.canada@primus.ca; www.kompas.net

## Europe

### *Austria*

**Kompas Touristik Reiseveranstaltung GmbH** Siebensterngasse 21, 1070 Vienna; tel: +43 01 402 2042; fax: +43 01 402 2825; email: kompasvie@via.at; www.kompas.net

## Benelux

**Kompas Holidays International BV** Benthuizerstraat 29 ben, 3036 CB Rotterdam, The Netherlands; tel: +31 010 465 7431; fax: +31 010 465 7514; email: kompasnl@euronet.nl; www.kompas.net

## France

**Kompas France International SA** 14 rue de la Source, 75016 Paris; tel: +33 01 53 92 27 80; fax: +33 01 42 15 20 52; email: parkompas@wanadoo.fr; www.kompas.net

## Germany

**Kompas International Reisen GmbH** Glienickerstrasse 40, 14109 Berlin; tel: +49 030 8060 2780; fax: +49 030 805 9037; email: kir@kompas-berlin.de; www.kompas.net

**Kompas International Reisen GmbH** Mainluststrasse 6/6, 60329 Frankfurt Am Main; tel: +49 069 233 024; fax: +49 069 236 945; email: info.fra@kompas.de; www.kompas.net

**Kompas International Reisen GmbH** Hochbruckenstrasse 10, 80331 Munich; tel: +49 089 904 6355; fax: +49 089 904 6253; email: info@kompas-muc.de; www.kompas.net

## Italy

**Kompas SRL** Piazza dell'Esquilino 8/G, 00185 Rome; tel: +39 06 4782 4267; fax: +39 06 4891 6042; email: kompas.rome@kompas.it; www.kompas.net

**Kompas SRL** S Marco 1497, 30124 Venice; tel: +39 04 1240 5600; fax: +39 04 1520 6184; email: kompas.venice@kompas.it; www.kompas.net

## *Russia*

**Kompas Representative Office** 3rd Tverskaja-Jamskaja St 24/1, 125047 Moscow; tel +70 095 251 3236; fax: +70 095 251 6795; email: kompas@cityline.ru; www.kompas.net

## *Scandinavia*

**Kompas Scandinavia** Enhojsparken 1, 3450 Allerod, Denmark; tel: +45 048 141 997; fax: +45 048 161 997; email: kompas.scandinavia@wanadoo.dk; www.kompas.net

## *Spain*

**Kompas Touristik Espana SA** Calle Valencia 494, Esc Dcha-A, 1°-2a, 08013 Barcelona; tel: +34 093 246 6777/5295; fax: +34 093 245 4188; email: incoming@kompas-spain.com; www.kompas.net

## *Switzerland*

**Kompas Travel Touroperating** Alpenstrasse 1, 6004 Lucerne; tel: +41 041 418 8030; fax: +41 041 418 8036



# RED TAPE

Although Slovenia joined the European Union on May 1 2004 it does not currently have Schengen border regulations. While the country is preparing for this it will not be eligible to join the Schengen zone until at least 2007. For most visitors Slovenia's border formalities are nominal and the majority simply need a valid passport for stays of less than three months. Citizens from EU countries and those from Croatia and Switzerland can enter Slovenia for up to 30 days with a national identity card.

Visa requirements for those travelling to Slovenia from a country that has not signed the Schengen agreement vary. At present those from Australia, New Zealand, Canada and the USA can stay for up to 90 days without a visa, while South Africans do need a visa. Visa requirements are subject to change and non-EU citizens are advised to check with the Slovenian Ministry of Foreign Affairs (www.sigov.si/mzz).

In accordance with EU regulations, citizens from EU member states can freely bring tobacco and alcohol into Slovenia for personal use. For non-EU members duty-free rules still apply. These restrict the import of tobacco to 200 cigarettes or 250g of tobacco or 50 cigars; 2l of wine, 1l of spirits, 50g of perfume and 250ml of eau de toilette can also be imported. Anyone entering Slovenia with more than 3 million SIT worth of cash or personal possessions needs to declare this on entry.

## SLOVENIAN EMBASSIES OVERSEAS

**Australia** Level 6, Advance Bank Center, 60 Marcus Clarke St, Canberra, ACT 2601; tel: +61 02 6243 4830; fax: +61 02 6243 4827

**Austria** Nibelungengasse 13, A-1010 Vienna; tel: +43 01 586 1309; fax: +43 01 586 1265; email: VDU@mzz-dkp.gov.si

**Belgium** Av Louise 179, B-1050 Brussels; tel: +32 02 646 9099; fax: +32 02 646 3667

**Canada** 150 Metcalfe St, Suite 2101, Ottawa, Ontario K2P 1P1; tel: +1 613 565 5781/2; fax: +1 613 565 5783; email: vot@mzz-dkp.gov.si

**Denmark** Amaliegade 6, 2nd floor, 1256 Copenhagen; tel: +45 33 730 120; fax: +45 33 150 607

**France** 28 rue Bois-le-Vent, 75116 Paris; tel: +33 01 44 96 50 66; fax: +33 01 45 24 67 05

**Germany** Hausvogteiplatz 3–4, D-10117 Berlin; tel: +49 030 206 145/0; fax: +49 030 206 145/70; email: VBO@mzz-dkp.gov.si

**Ireland** Morrison Chambers, 2nd Floor, Nassau St, Dublin 2; tel: +353 01 670 5240; fax: +353 01 670 5243; email: vdb@mzz-dkp.gov.si; www.gov.si/mzz/dkp/vdb

**Italy** Via Leonardo Pisano 10, I-00197 Rome; tel: +39 06 8091 4310; fax: +39 06 8081 471; email: VRI@mzz-dkp.gov.si

**New Zealand** PO Box 30247, Lower Hutt, Wellington; tel: +64 04 567 0027; fax: +64 04 567 0024

**Russia** ul Mala Dimitrovka (Čehova) 14/1, 103006 Moscow; tel: +70 95 209 0203 or +75 03 737 3398; fax: +70 095 200 1568

**Spain** Hermanos Becquer 7-2, 28006 Madrid; tel: +34 091 411 6893; fax: +34 091 564 6057

**Switzerland** Schwanengasse 9/II, CH-3011 Bern; tel: +41 031 311 4421; fax: +41 031 312 4414; email: VBE@mzz-dkp.gov.si

**UK** 10 Little College St, London SW1P 3SJ; tel: +44 020 7222 5400; fax: +44 020 7222 5277; email: VLO@mzz-dkp.gov.si; www.slovenia.embassyhomepage.com

**USA** 1525 New Hampshire Av NW, Washington, DC 20036; tel: +1 202 667 5363; fax: +1 202 667 4563; email: slovenia@embassy.org; www.embassy.org/slovenia

# GETTING THERE AND AWAY

## By air

Ljubljana's Brnik Airport, located 23km northwest of the city centre, is relatively small by European standards. Facilities in the departures hall are better than in arrivals (where annoyingly there is not even an ATM), with an ATM, car rental, currency exchange, bar, telephone-operated hotel booking system, restaurants, telephones, toilets and shops. The airport terminal is well served by taxis and bus services. Six scheduled airlines serve Brnik providing the city with direct connections to more than 20 destinations worldwide including Amsterdam, Belgrade, Berlin, Brussels, Budapest, Copenhagen, Dublin, Frankfurt, Istanbul, London (Stansted and Gatwick), Manchester, Moscow, Munich, Ohrid, Paris, Podgorica, Prague, Pristina, Sarajevo, Skopje, Split, Tel Aviv, Tirana, Vienna and Zürich.

**Ljubljana Brnik Airport** Tel: 04 206 1981; fax: 04 206 1109; email: info@lju-airport.si; www.lju-airport.si

**Adria Airways** Tel: 04 259 4245; www.adria-airways.com

**Austrian Airlines** Tel: 01 239 1900; www.aua-si.com

**Czech Airlines** Tel: 04 206 1750; www.czechairlines.com

**easyJet** Tel: 04 206 1677; www.easyJet.com

**JAT Airways** Tel: 04 206 1780; www.jat.com

**Malév** Tel: 04 206 1676; www.malev.hu

The introduction of easyJet flights from London Stansted to Ljubljana in April 2004 provided the city with its first low-cost carrier. EasyJet added a direct Berlin connection later in 2004 and a Basel–Ljubljana route early in 2005. Adria Airways operates twice-weekly direct flights from Dublin to Ljubljana during the summer season. Those who are seeking to keep the costs down might also consider flying with Ryanair to Trieste, 110km from Ljubljana, or Klagenfurt, 79km away. If you are planning to do this it is essential to consider the cost of onward travel from these destinations. Another alternative is to catch a charter flight to Slovenia's other international airports in Portorož and Maribor (though currently there are no scheduled services).

**Ronchi dei Legionari Trieste Ariport** Via Aquileia 46, 34077 Ronchi dei Legionari, Italy; tel: +39 04 8177 3224; fax: +39 04 8147 4150; email: info@aeroporto.fvg.it; www.aeroporto.fvg.it

**Klagenfurt** Flughafenstraße 60–66, A-9020 Klagenfurt, Austria; tel: +43 04 634 1500; email: info@klagenfurt-airport.at; www.klagenfurt-airport.com

**Ryanair** tel: +353 01 249 7851 (European reservations are charged at international rates); www.ryanair.com

## By train

Slovenian Railways, whose network connects the country to the rest of Europe via Germany, Italy, Austria, Switzerland, Hungary and Greece, as well as countries that were formerly part of Yugoslavia, operate Slovenia's train services. Ljubljana's train station is located on the edge of the city centre and is well served by domestic and international rail services. International trains include the *Mimara* which connects Munich, Salzburg, Villach, Jesenice and Zagreb to Ljubljana. The *Emona* travels from Vienna via Graz and Maribor to the city, whilst the *Simplon Express* operates between Geneva and Zagreb via Ljubljana and the *Drava Express* runs between Budapest and Venice via Ljubljana. The new high-speed *Casanova* serves Venice (Mestre and Santa Lucia) once daily, missing out the Trieste switchback, and cutting journey times by around 90 minutes to four hours.

**Railway station (Železniška postaja)** Trg Osvobodilne fronte 6; tel: 01 291 3332; email: potnik.info@slo-zeleznice.si; www.slo-zeleznice.si [1 E2] **C**

**Slovenian Railways (Slovenske železnice)** tel: 01 291 3332; email: potnik.info@slo-zeleznice.si; www.slo-zeleznice.si

## By bus

Located in the centre of town, Ljubljana's bus station is served by an extensive number of national and international services, with connections to destinations all over Slovenia and neighbouring Croatia. There are also a large number of services operating to the other states in the former Yugoslavia – Bosnia-Herzegovina, Macedonia, Serbia and Montenegro. International services also link the Slovenian capital to Austria, Hungary, Denmark, Sweden, Germany, France, Belgium and Italy.

**Bus station (Avtobusna postaja)** Trg Osvobodilne fronte 4; tel: 090 4230; email: avtobusna.postaja@ap-ljubljana.si; www.ap-ljubljana.si [1 E2] **C**

## By car

Ljubljana is easily accessible by car from mainland Europe. The key routes used by drivers travelling from Austria include the E651 which links Ljubljana to Villach, the E652/E61 from Klagenfurt and the E57/E59 from Graz. From Italy the E61/E70 connects Trieste to Ljubljana, whilst the E70 serves Zagreb in neighbouring Croatia and the E57/E71 extends to Budapest in Hungary. If you are planning to travel to Ljubljana from Great Britain you will obviously have to cross either the North Sea or the English Channel first, with the former providing the most direct route.

### *Road distances from Ljubljana*

Klagenfurt 79km; Trieste 110km; Zagreb 135km; Graz 202km; Venice 249km; Salzburg 290km; Vienna 395km; Munich 430km; Budapest 491km; and Belgrade 507km.

## By sea

Ljubljana does not have a port, but marinas in Portorož, Izola and Koper have facilities for yachts. During the tourist season two passenger catamaran services, the Prince of Venice and Venezia Lines, run between Venice and the Slovenian coast. Prince of Venice services operate from March to October, shuttling passengers between Venice and Izola (approximate journey time 2½ hours; prices 9,800–15,500SIT). Ticket prices for this service include a guided tour of Venice and can be purchased from Kompas travel agents in Slovenia.

The Venezia Lines service from Venice docks at Piran. Tickets for this service can be purchased from Atlas Express travel agents and cost around 10,800SIT for a single ticket and 19,200SIT return. If you arrive in Slovenia at either Izola or Piran you can take a local bus to Koper from where regular train and bus services leave for the capital.

**Marina Portorož** Cesta solinarjev 8, 6320 Portorož; tel: 05 676 1100; fax: 05 676 1210; email: marina.portoroz@marinap.si; www.marinap.si
**Marina Izola** Tomažičeva 10, 6310 Izola; tel: 05 640 0250; fax: 05 641 8346; email: info@marinaizola.com; www.marinaizola.com
**Marina Koper** Kopališko nabrežje 5, 6000 Koper; tel: 05 662 6100; fax: 05 662 6161; email: info@marina-koper.si; www.marina-koper.si
**Kompas** (For Prince of Venice services) PE Portorož, Obala 41, 6320 Portorož; tel: 05 617 8000; fax: 05 674 7258; email: portoroz@kompas.si; www.kompas-holy.si
**Venezia Lines** tel: +39 04 1520 5473; fax: +39 04 1277 8335; email: info@venezialines.com; www.venezialines.com

## HEALTH

It is safe to drink tap water throughout Slovenia and visitors travelling to the country do not need any special inoculations. However, it is wise to be up-to-date with primary courses and boosters as recommended in the UK, in particular for diphtheria, tetanus and polio. For those who are intending to work in the healthcare setting or are working closely with children, hepatitis B vaccination is recommended. Also those with special needs such as the elderly should consider influenza and pneumococcal vaccine. Typhoid vaccine is not usually recommended for travellers.

Ljubljana's health centres are generally open Monday–Friday 07.00–19.00, and its pharmacies (*lekarna*) open 07.00–20.00. If you urgently require medication the prescribing doctor should be able to help you find a reasonably close 24-hour pharmacy (see *Hospitals/pharmacies*).

Emergency medical care for EU citizens is free upon the production of a valid E111 form (European Health Insurance Cards are being phased in to replace the E111 forms, a process that started on June 1 2004) or other appropriate documentation; for UK citizens a passport is sufficient, as long as treatment is given in a state-funded hospital or health centre. However, it is wise to have medical insurance just in case. If you are a UK resident but not a UK national a certificate of insurance is needed. This is obtainable from the Inland Revenue Contributions Office, International Services, Longbenton, Newcastle-upon-Tyne NE98 1ZZ. Other non-emergency treatment or consultations and medicine must be paid for. Citizens of Croatia, Romania and Bulgaria are also entitled to free emergency medical care in Slovenia.

Visitors from countries that do not have a reciprocal medical agreement with Slovenia must pay for all of their medical care, including emergency care. Your national Ministry for Health can tell you if any mutual agreements exist.

Regardless of any health agreements that may be in place, all international visitors to Slovenia should take out travel insurance with an adequate level of medical cover before travelling to the country. This is important in case you need emergency repatriation.

A few simple precautions, before you leave for Slovenia, will help you safeguard your health during your trip. If you take prescribed medication make sure you pack it and keep a separate note of the drug's proper name and not just its brand. This will make replacement easier. Those who are travelling for a long time should consider going for a dental check-up. Taking an adequate supply of contact lenses or a spare pair of glasses is also advisable.

In Ljubljana itself the biggest risk to your health is the sun. The city can get surprisingly hot during the summer, making it essential to pack light clothing that allows your skin to breathe, sunglasses that provide UV protection, a sunhat and plenty of suntan lotion. If you forget any of these items you will be able to buy them in the city.

Those who are intending to travel away from the capital need to consider the following health risks:

**Tick-borne encephalitis** is a viral infection, transmitted by ticks found in densely forested parts of Slovenia, which affects the central nervous system. It is possible to vaccinate against the disease, though this is not generally recommended for those at low risk, such as day-trippers. If you are planning on spending a prolonged period of time in a forested area you should seek appropriate medical advice before leaving. Other precautionary measures include avoiding tick-infested areas from April through to August when the risk of infection is at its highest, wearing clothing that covers your skin or wearing an insect repellent containing DEET (diethyl-m-toluamide). Permethrin-based insect repellents can also be applied to your clothing and camping gear, although this should never be put on to your skin. These repellent agents are also effective against Slovenian mosquitoes, which can give you painful bites but do not carry malaria. Following any trip into forested areas you should check carefully for ticks and if present remove carefully with tweezers taking care not to damage the mouth part. (If you are unsure about doing this yourself a medical professional will do it for you.) Then go as soon as possible to a doctor as there is treatment available following exposure. You can also get tick-borne encephalitis from unpasteurised dairy products and these should be avoided.

**Lyme disease** is a bacterial infection transmitted by ticks that have fed on an infected host animal. Again the risk of infection is at its highest in forested areas between April and August and the same preventative precautions described for tick-borne encephalitis should be taken except that there is no vaccine available for this disease. Symptoms associated with Lyme disease include a red abrasion at the site where the tick bit, which can be up to 7.5cm in diameter and is often clear in the centre. Fever, headaches, a stiff neck, muscular pain, inflamed joints and extreme lethargy are amongst the symptoms.

**Hepatitis A** is a virus that attacks the human liver and, while it is rare, can affect anyone. After an incubation period of three to five weeks, infected individuals display flu-like symptoms and experience fever, abdominal pains, nausea, lack of appetite, lethargy and jaundice. The length of illness and convalescence varies and can be prolonged, but the majority of patients make a complete recovery. The disease is transmitted through food or water contaminated with human faeces, so it is essential to maintain a high level of personal hygiene when travelling. Restaurants in Ljubljana conform to high standards, so visitors do not normally need to worry about what they are eating or drinking. Hikers or climbers intending to drink fresh water from streams should either boil it or treat it with purifying tablets. If you have any doubts about the quality of the water that you are drinking opt for bottled mineral water. Vaccination against Hepatitis A is recommended for those who travel frequently or are intending to spend time outside Ljubjlana. Injections are administered in two stages with the second dose being given six months after the first. Those who have already suffered with hepatitis A are immune from the disease.

**Rabies** is a viral disease transmitted in the saliva of an infected animal in the form of a bite, scratch or a lick over an open wound. Although they are extremely rare, incidences of rabies do occur in Slovenia. The best defence against rabies is prevention, making it essential to avoid handling wild or stray animals. However, if you think you have been exposed, wash the area immediately with soap and water and apply an antiseptic. Seek medical help as soon as possible as post-exposure rabies vaccine, if given promptly, will prevent disease. For any visitor who intends to work with animals it is important to receive pre-exposure rabies vaccine. Three doses given over a minimum of 21 days is ideal. Likewise those spending four weeks or more outside Ljubljana may wish to consider this option. Remember that rabies if untreated is always fatal!

## Travel clinics and health information

A full list of current travel clinic websites worldwide is available on www.istm.org/. For other journey preparation information, consult www.tripprep.com. Information about various medications may be found on www.emedicine.com/wild/topiclist.htm.

### *UK*

**Berkeley Travel Clinic** 32 Berkeley St, London W1J 8EL (near Green Park tube station); tel: 020 7629 6233

**British Airways Travel Clinic and Immunisation Service** There are two BA clinics in London, both on tel: 0845 600 2236; www.britishairways.com/travelclinics. Appointments only at 111 Cheapside; or walk-in service Mon–Sat at 156 Regent St. Apart from providing inoculations and malaria prevention, they sell a variety of health-related goods.

**The Travel Clinic, Cambridge** 48a Mill Rd, Cambridge CB1 2AS; tel: 01223 367362; fax: 01223 368021; email: enquiries@travelcliniccambridge.co.uk; www.travelcliniccambridge.co.uk. Open 12.00–19.00 Tue–Fri, 10.00–16.00 Sat.

**Edinburgh Travel Clinic** Regional Infectious Diseases Unit, Ward 41 OPD, Western General Hospital, Crewe Rd South, Edinburgh EH4 2UX; tel: 0131 537 2822. Travel helpline open 09.00–12.00 weekdays. Provides inoculations and anti-malarial prophylaxis and advises on travel-related health risks.

**Fleet Street Travel Clinic** 29 Fleet St, London EC4Y 1AA; tel: 020 7353 5678; www.fleetstreet.com. Injections, travel products and latest advice.

**Hospital for Tropical Diseases Travel Clinic** Mortimer Market Centre, 2nd Floor, Capper St (off Tottenham Ct Rd), London WC1E 6AU; tel: 020 7388 9600; www.thhtd.org. Offers consultations and advice, and is able to provide all necessary drugs and vaccines for travellers. Runs a healthline (tel: 09061 337733) for country-specific information and health hazards. Also stocks nets, water purification equipment and personal protection measures.

**MASTA** (Medical Advisory Service for Travellers Abroad), at the London School of Hygiene and Tropical Medicine, Keppel St, London WC1 7HT; tel: 09068 224100. This is a premium-line number, charged at 60p per minute. For a fee, they will provide an individually tailored health brief, with up-to-date information on how to stay healthy, inoculations and what to bring.

**MASTA pre-travel clinics** Tel: 01276 685040. Call for the nearest; there are currently 30 in Britain. Also sell malaria prophylaxis memory cards, treatment kits, bednets, net treatment kits.

**NHS travel website** www.fitfortravel.scot.nhs.uk. Provides country-by-country advice on immunisation and malaria, plus details of recent developments, and a list of relevant health organisations.

**Nomad Travel Store** 3–4 Wellington Terrace, Turnpike Lane, London N8 0PX; tel: 020 8889 7014; fax: 020 8889 9528; email: sales@nomadtravel.co.uk; www.nomadtravel.co.uk. Also at 40 Bernard St, London WC1N 1LJ; tel: 020 7833 4114; fax: 020 7833 4470 and 43 Queens Rd, Bristol BS8 1QH; tel: 0117 922 6567; fax: 0117 922 7789. As well as dispensing health advice, Nomad stocks mosquito nets and other anti-bug devices, and an excellent range of adventure travel gear.

**Thames Medical** 157 Waterloo Rd, London SE1 8US; tel: 020 7902 9000. Competitively priced, one-stop travel health service. All profits go to their affiliated company, InterHealth, which provides health care for overseas workers on Christian projects.

**Trailfinders Immunisation Centre** 194 Kensington High St, London W8 7RG; tel: 020 7938 3999.

**Travelpharm** The Travelpharm website, www.travelpharm.com, offers up-to-date guidance on travel-related health and has a range of medications available through their online mini-pharmacy.

## *Irish Republic*

**Tropical Medical Bureau** Grafton Street Medical Centre, Grafton Buildings, 34 Grafton St, Dublin 2; tel: 1 671 9200. Has a useful website specific to tropical destinations: www.tmb.ie.

## *USA*

**Centers for Disease Control** 1600 Clifton Rd, Atlanta, GA 30333; tel: 888 232 3228 (toll free and available 24 hours) or 800 311 3435; fax: 877 FYI TRIP; www.cdc.gov/travel. The central source of travel information in the USA. Each summer they publish the invaluable *Health Information for International Travel*, available from the Division of Quarantine at the above address.

**Connaught Laboratories** PO Box 187, Swiftwater, PA 18370; tel: 800 822 2463. They will send a free list of specialist tropical-medicine physicians in your state.

**IAMAT** (International Association for Medical Assistance to Travelers) 417 Center St, Lewiston, NY 14092; tel: 716 754 4883; email: info@iamat.org; www.iamat.org. A non-profit organisation that provides lists of English-speaking doctors abroad.

## *Canada*

**IAMAT** (International Association for Medical Assistance to Travellers) Suite 1, 1287 St Clair Av W, Toronto, Ontario M6E 1B8; tel: 416 652 0137; www.iamat.org

**TMVC** (Travel Doctors Group) Sulphur Springs Rd, Ancaster, Ontario; tel: 905 648 1112; www.tmvc.com.au

## *Australia, New Zealand, Thailand*

**TMVC** Tel: 1300 65 88 44; www.tmvc.com.au. Twenty-two clinics in Australia, New Zealand and Thailand, including:

*Auckland* Canterbury Arcade, 170 Queen St, Auckland; tel: 9 373 3531

*Brisbane* Dr Deborah Mills, Qantas Domestic Building, 6th floor, 247 Adelaide St, Brisbane, QLD 4000; tel: 7 3221 9066; fax: 7 3321 7076

*Melbourne* Dr Sonny Lau, 393 Little Bourke St, 2nd floor, Melbourne, VIC 3000; tel: 3 9602 5788; fax: 3 9670 8394

*Sydney* Dr Mandy Hu, Dymocks Building, 7th Floor, 428 George St, Sydney, NSW 2000; tel: 2 221 7133; fax: 2 221 8401

**IAMAT** PO Box 5049, Christchurch 5, New Zealand; www.iamat.org

### South Africa

**SAA-Netcare Travel Clinics** PO Box 786692, Sandton 2146; fax: 011 883 6152; www.travelclinic.co.za or www.malaria.co.za. Clinics throughout South Africa.

**TMVC** 113 DF Malan Drive, Roosevelt Park, Johannesburg; tel: 011 888 7488; www.tmvc.com.au. Consult the website for details of clinics in South Africa.

### Switzerland

**IAMAT** 57 Voirets, 1212 Grand Lancy, Geneva; www.iamat.org

## SAFETY

Ljubljana is a safe city with a low crime rate, especially when compared to cities in other western European countries and violent crimes are rare. Travellers should, though, take sensible precautions to safeguard their valuables as tourists occasionally fall prey to pickpockets and handbag snatchers. Simple measures, such as not leaving valuables in unattended cars, keeping purses and wallets in inside pockets, carrying bags securely and facing away from the road are all effective deterrents against crime. Anyone unfortunate enough to become a victim of crime should report it to the police immediately – this is especially important if you intend to make a travel insurance claim when you return home.

## WOMEN TRAVELLERS

Ljubljana is a modern city with a youthful population and female travellers should not experience any specific difficulties. Again sensible precautions should be taken to avoid potentially dangerous situations, like not meeting strange men in secluded places. The usual precautions should also be taken against sexually transmitted diseases.

## GAY AND LESBIAN TRAVELLERS

The gay and lesbian scene in Ljubljana is not as prominent as in many European cities, but there is one, and while attitudes towards homosexuality amongst the older generation are often far from enlightened, being gay or lesbian is becoming more socially acceptable. Although attitudes are improving in Ljubljana, public displays of affection between gay and lesbian couples are not the norm.

The first Ljubljana Gay and Lesbian Pride Parade was staged in 2000, and this annual event has been credited with helping change attitudes in the city. In addition the gay and lesbian communities in Ljubljana showed that they were not willing to be pushed around during the 'water protest' a few years ago when the new owner of Galerija decided to axe it as a gay bar. For months the local gay community showed its resolve by occupying the money-spinning outdoor tables and ordering only water. (See *Gay Listings* in the *Entertainment and Nightlife* chapter for details of the city's gay and gay-friendly venues.)

## WHAT TO TAKE

Ljubljana is a modern, cosmopolitan city where you can buy anything that you might need. Your only essentials are a valid passport or acceptable national identity card, a visa if necessary, transport tickets, travel insurance documents, money (debit or credit cards, travellers' cheques or Slovenian tolars), E111 or other documentation showing an entitlement to healthcare, driving licence (national or international depending on country-specific requirements), student discount cards and an international youth hostel membership card. Keep photocopies of important documents such as passports, visas and travel insurance policies in case they need to be replaced.

It is advisable to pack for the weather, sticking to light clothes that let your skin breathe in the summer, with sunscreen, sunglasses and a hat all essential items. In the winter you will need a warm and waterproof coat, and a lighter jacket in the spring and autumn. It is also sensible to take a light waterproof raincoat or an umbrella at any time of year. Ljubljana has a buzzing nightlife, so you might want to pack your favourite clubbing gear. Anyone intending to dine out in the city's more expensive restaurants should pack smart casual clothes, though formal wear is not normally required except for specific business functions.



## MONEY AND BUDGETING

### Currency

The official currency of Slovenia is the delightfully colourful Slovenian tolar (SIT), with around 240SIT to the euro and 350SIT to the British pound. The tolar is a decimal currency and there are 100 stotins in a tolar, however you will rarely come across these. Tolar notes, brightly bedecked with images of great Slovene painters, writers and thinkers rather than monarchs and politicians in a refreshing change, come in denominations of 5,000, 1,000, 500, 200, 100, 50 and 20. There are also one, two, five and ten tolar coins. With large figures representing small amounts of money you can end up with a substantial wad of notes in your pocket, so be careful when pulling them out.

## Budgeting

Home to Slovenia's biggest university, a large business community and a growing number of expatriates, you can spend as little or as much as you want to in Ljubljana. Regardless of your budget there are a couple of things to bear in mind. Firstly hotel accommodation is pricey and in short supply, though costs are significantly less if you are travelling with a partner or friends, as double, triple and quadruple rooms work out cheaper. If you are planning on visiting a lot of the city's museums then purchasing the Ljubljana Card for 3,000SIT, valid for 72 hours, is a good investment. If you are staying in a hotel outside the centre it also gives free bus transport.

### *Rock bottom*

You can get by on 7,000SIT a day in Ljubljana if you camp or stay in a youth hostel dormitory and buy food from the central market or fast-food stands. This budget will also allow you to eat one meal in a pizzeria or student eatery and to buy drinks from a supermarket. If you are planning to travel on a tight budget it is essential that you book your accommodation in advance.

## Modest

Being savvy about where you stay will allow you to eat two meals in modestly priced, but good quality, restaurants and enjoy four or five drinks in the city's cafés and bars for 12,000–19,000SIT. Again if you want to keep your accommodation costs down then it is advisable to book a hostel or private room in advance. The latter figure would allow you to stay in a single room at the fairly centrally located two-star Park Hotel or a room rather than a dorm at the Celica Hostel.

## Fun

For around 30,000SIT you can afford single occupancy in one of Ljubljana's more affordable three-star hotels, eat two reasonably priced meals and not have to worry about what you drink.

## Indulgent

Spend 45,000SIT a day and stay in any of the city's three-star hotels, or some of the four-star hotels, and eat out twice, choosing from the majority of Ljubljana's restaurants. You will also be able to pay the entrance fee to the sights of your choice and enjoy a night out.

### *Extravagant*
From 65,000SIT upwards you will be able to stay in one of the city's four- or five-star hotels, eat in its most exclusive restaurants and spend the day as you choose such as relaxing in cafés, drinking in bars, sightseeing or taking a river cruise. Again a budget of this size means that you can go out at night without having to watch the tolars.

### *Tipping*
In restaurants and hotels it is usual to leave a 10% tip, unless the service has been really poor. Taxi drivers will also expect a tip.

## BUSINESS
Since becoming independent in 1991 Slovenia has quickly established itself as an efficient and stable democracy and businesses in Slovenia generally operate to the same standards as other western European countries. Its recent accession to the EU is expected to boost trade with other member states and to attract more international investors.

For those conducting business in Slovenia a few common courtesies will ensure that everything runs smoothly: these include wearing smart business dress, being punctual for meetings and keeping an ample supply of business cards. The majority of Ljubljana's businesspeople are fluent in English, with many also speaking German and Italian. Office hours are Monday–Friday 08.00–16.00, but business is often conducted over lunch or dinner.

The Slovenian Chamber of Commerce and Industry (www.gzs.si), the website InvestSlovenia – Tipo (www.investslovenia.org), Slovenia Business Week (www.gzs.si/eng/news/sbw) and commercial advisors at foreign embassies in Slovenia can all provide useful information about doing business in Ljubljana.

Slovenia is an increasingly popular destination for MICE events. All of Ljubljana's four- and five-star hotels have conference and business facilities, including the luxurious Lev hotel, the high-tech Domina Grand Media and the Mons Hotel and Congress Centre, the city's newest hotel and Ljubljana's first design hotel, which opened in September 2004. For larger groups the Cankarjev Dom Congress and Cultural Centre (www.cd-cc.si) has ten halls, which can accommodate a maximum of 1,400 delegates, and four additional conference rooms. The Grand Union Hotel (www.gh-union.si) also have dedicated conference facilities. Specialist staff at the Slovenian Tourist Board are also on hand to help you arrange an event (www.slovenia-tourism.si).

## CULTURAL DOS AND DON'TS

### Dos

Slovenes consider it polite to shake hands with someone, especially when meeting them for the first time. Those on business are also expected to exchange business cards. Also when clinking glasses and toasting, say '*Nazdravje*' (pronounced *noz-drav-yee*) and make sure you look everyone in the eye, then take a sip before returning your glass to the table.

## Don'ts

Slovenes expect the same standards of behaviour in public as other western European countries. It is also illegal to smoke in cinemas, theatres and waiting rooms, or on public transport. Be polite and considerate to cyclists as cycling is part of the culture and you will seldom win an argument with anyone on two wheels even if they have just tried to cut you in half on a pedestrian crossing.

3

# Practicalities

## BANKS AND MONEY MATTERS

### Banks

You won't have to walk far to find a bank in the centre of Ljubljana. Most open Monday–Friday 08.30–12.30 and 14.00–17.00 and Saturdays 08.30–12.00, though not all branches open on Saturdays and some open all day during the week. Most banks accept cash or travellers' cheques.

### Currency exchange

Cash can also be exchanged in post offices, exchange offices, hotels, some petrol stations, tourist agencies and even supermarkets; the same outlets will not necessarily accept travellers' cheques.

### Credit cards/debit cards

American Express, Diners Club, Mastercard/Eurocard and Visa credit cards and Visa, Electron, Plus, Maestro and Cirrus debit cards are accepted in most shops, restaurants and hotels. It is also possible to withdraw cash from most ATMs using either your credit or debit card, as long as you have a valid PIN number. With the majority of cards you can also withdraw money inside the bank if you don't know your PIN or the ATM is broken. Fees charged for cash withdrawals and exchange rates vary between bank and credit card companies, so check these before you leave home. Transaction charges on credit and debit cards can be kept down by withdrawing larger sums of money, although there will be an upper limit on the amount you can extract.

If you are travelling with credit cards it is sensible to keep a record of the issuer's international telephone number for reporting lost or stolen cards. In the case of loss or theft your credit card company should help you arrange emergency cash if necessary. You can also get assistance with damaged, lost or stolen cards in Ljubljana.

**American Express** tel: 433 2024
**Diners Club** tel: 589 61111
**Mastercard/Eurocard** tel: 425 0155 or 433 2132
**Visa** tel: 431 1031

### Travellers' cheques

Travellers' cheques are much safer than carrying cash. Euro or US$ travellers' cheques can be exchanged at banks, exchange offices, travel agencies and some post offices. Banks offer the best rate with commissions ranging from zero to 1%. Remember that you will need a valid passport to cash your cheques.

## MEDIA

### Press

Slovenia has four daily newspapers, which are printed in Slovenia and available on the internet (see *Further reading*), the Ljubljana-based *Delo* (Work), *Dnevnik*

(Daily) and *Ljubljanske Novice*, and the Maribor-based *Večer* (Evening). There is also a diverse range of weekly, fortnightly and monthly newspapers and magazines on sale.

English-language publications take the form of the weekly *Slovenia News*, the monthly *Slovenia Times*, the quarterly *Ljubljana Life*, whose website contains the *Slovenia Bulletin* (a weekly review of the stories in Slovenia's mainstream press), and the quarterly *Slovenija Magazine*. Sources of business news include the quarterly *Slovenian Business Report* (Slovene language) and the online *Slovenia Business Week* (English language). In addition the government's *Public Relations and Media Office* is an official source of English-language news (see *Further reading*).

*The Guardian International*, *International Herald Tribune*, *USA Today* and *The Financial Times* are also widely available in hotels, bookshops and at kiosks throughout Ljubljana.

## Radio

*Radiotelevizija Slovenija* (RTV Slovenia) broadcast radio and television programmes in Slovenia. RTV Slovenia (www.rtvslo.si) transmits three national radio channels, regional channels that include tourist broadcasts in foreign languages and one channel each for the country's Italian and Hungarian minorities. Around 100 radio stations in Slovenia also transmit commercial and non-commercial programmes. Tourist Radio (Turistični radio) is available on 87.6MHz, 89.2MHz, 91.1MHz, 102.4MHz and 102.8MHz.

## TV

RTV Slovenia broadcasts Slovenia's two national television channels and two regional channels – Koper-Capodistia in Koper and another in Maribor. Pro Plus operate the commercial channels Kanal A and Pop TV, which air a mixture of domestic and international programmes, while TV3 has a mixed Croatian–Slovene ownership. Most of Ljubljana's better hotels have CNN, BBC World and other satellite channels like Discovery, MTV and Eurosport.

# COMMUNICATIONS

## Internet cafés

Home internet use is widespread in Slovenia so few locals need internet cafés, however there is still a sprinkling of places to get online. Many hotels and hostels also provide internet points for guests. The new Slovenian Tourist Information Centre (TIC) at Krekov trg 10 [3 E5] **C** offers half an hour of high-speed access for 250SIT. Alternatively if you have a Hotmail or Yahoo account you can check your emails at the information point in the Ljubljana Tourist Information Centre on Stritarjeva [3 D5] **C** by the Triple Bridge, a service which should be used considerately as the machine's primary function is to provide your fellow travellers with information about Ljubljana and Slovenia. Other options include:

**Napotnica.com** Trg Ajdovščina 1; tel: 431 1016; www.napotnica.com [1 C4] **C**
You will find this friendly and central cyber café on the upper level of a small shopping centre on the corner of Slovenska and Dalmatinova. Rate 800SIT per hour.

**Cyber Café Xplorer** Petkovškovo nabrežje 23; tel: 430 1991; www.sisky.com [1 E4] **C**
This professional internet café has fast machines and add-ons like webcams and DVD. Terminals are housed in private booths, with a soft drinks machine available if you are feeling thirsty. The minimum five minutes comes in at 110SIT and rates rise through to 860SIT an hour. Student discounts apply.

**Čerin** Trubarjeva 52; tel: 232 0990 [2 F4] **OCC**
Free internet is available at this pizzeria so you can munch on some of the city's finest pizza while you surf.

**DrogArt** Kolodvorska 20; tel: 439 7270 [1 E2] **C**
Located opposite the railway station with no charge for the first 15 minutes. Maximum usage time is one hour and costs 400SIT.

**Grostilna Nobile** Zarnikova 3; tel: 439 7040 [4 G6] **OCC**
Suburban eatery with two internet terminals.

## Post offices

The post office at Slovenska 32 [1 C4] **C** is open Monday–Friday 07.00–20.00 and Saturday 08.00–13.00 while the branch at Trg Osvobodilne fronte 5 [1 E2] **C** opens Monday–Friday 07.00–midnight, Saturday 07.00–18.00 and Sunday 09.00–12.00. Post office services include stamps, telegrams and magnetic phonecards.

## Telephones

*Telekom Slovenije* (www.telekom.si) operates the country's telephone network and has a useful online directory available in Slovene and English. Only magnetic phonecards *(telekartica)* can be used in Ljubljana's public phones; these cost 700–3,500SIT and are sold at post offices and some newspaper kiosks.

### *Dialling*

The international dialling code for Slovenia is 386 and the Ljubljana city code is 01. To call Ljubljana from outside Slovenia dial the exit code of the country you are in, followed by the country code for Slovenia (386) and then the code for Ljubljana, omitting the 0, before dialling the rest of the nine-digit number. To call Ljubljana from inside Slovenia dial the city code in full. Calls made within Ljubljana do not need the 01 code. If you want to make an overseas phone call from Slovenia the country's exit code is 00.

### *Useful telephone numbers*

**Police** 113
**Fire** 112
**Medical emergency** 112
**Automobile Association of Slovenia (AMZS)** 1987
**Directory enquiries** 1188
**International directory enquiries** 1180

**International operator** 115
**General information** 090 93 9881
**Alarm call** 198 10
**Time (in Slovene)** 195

## EMBASSIES/CONSULATES IN LJUBLJANA

Not all embassies/consulates have websites or public email addresses.

**Australia** (Consulate) Trg Republike 3/XII; tel: 425 4252; fax: 426 4721 [3 B5] **C**
**Austria** Prešernova 23; tel: 479 0700; fax: 252 1717; email: austroamb@austrianembassy.si; www.austriantrade.si [1 B4] **C**
**Belgium** Trg Republike 3/IX; tel: 200 6010 [3 B5] **C**
**Canada** (Consulate) Miklošičeva 19; tel: 430 3570; fax: 430 3575 [1 D4] **C**
**Denmark** Eurocentre, Tivolski 48; tel: 438 0800 [off map] **OCC**
**EU** Trg Republike 3/XI; tel: 425 1303 [3 B5] **C**
**France** Barjanska 1; tel: 479 0400 [3 C7] **KT**
**Germany** Prešernova 27; tel: 479 0300; fax: 425 0899 [1 B4] **C**
**Ireland** Palača Kapitelj, Poljanski nasip 6; tel: 300 8970; fax: 282 1096; email: irish.embassy@siol.net [4 F5] **C**
**Italy** Snežniška 8; tel: 426 2194; fax: 425 3302; email: amblubiana@siol.net [3 A5] **OCC**
**New Zealand** (Consulate) Verovškova 57; tel: 580 3055; fax: 568 3526; email: janja.bratos@lek.si [off map] **OCC**
**Russia** Tomišičeva 9; tel: 425 6875 [1 B4] **C**

**South Africa** (Consulate) Pražakova 4; tel: 200 6300; fax: 200 6434 [1 D2] **C**
**Spain** Trnovski pristan 24; tel: 425 6875 [3 D8] **KT**
**Switzerland** Trg Republike 3/VI; tel: 200 8640 [3 B5] **C**
**UK** Trg Republike 3/IV; tel: 200 3910; fax: 425 0174; email: info@british-embassy.sil; www.british-embassy.si [3 B5] **C**
**USA** Prešernova 31; tel: 200 5500; fax: 200 5555; email: email@usembassy.si; www.usembassy.si [1 B4] **C**

## HOSPITALS/PHARMACIES

Ljubljana's **hospital** (*Klinični Centre Ljubljana*) is located at Zaloška 2; tel: 552 5050 [2 H4] **OCC**. There is also an emergency medical centre (*Urgenca Klinični Centre*) at Bohoričeva 4; tel: 552 8408 [2 J3] **OCC** and a dentist at Kotnikova 36; tel: 425 4061 [2 F3] **OCC**. For non-emergency medical care, or to find one of the city's many **pharmacies** (*lekarna*), seek advice where you are staying or at a tourist information centre. Centrally located pharmacies are at Milošičeva 24 [1 D4] **C** and Prešernov trg 1 [1 D4] **C**.

## RELIGIOUS SERVICES

In keeping with the religious beliefs of the majority of its population most of the church services in Ljubljana are Roman Catholic. Service times included in this listing are for Sundays only. The tourist information centre can provide information about Ljubljana's other places of worship and religious services held during the week.

**Stolna Cerkev Sv Nikolaja** (St Nicholas's Cathedral) Dolničarjeva 1; tel: 234 2690 [3 D3:E3] **OT**
Services: 06.00, 07.00, 08.00, 09.00, 10.30, 11.30, 12.30, 16.00 and 18.30

**Frančiškanska Cerkev Marijinega Oznanjenja** (Franciscan Church of the Annunciation) Prešernov trg 4; tel: 242 9300 [1 D4] **C**
Services: 07.00, 08.00, 09.00, 11.00, 16.00, 19.00 and 21.00

**Srbska Pravoslavna Cerkev** (Serbian Orthodox Church) Prešernova; tel: 252 4002 [1 B4] **C**
Service: 10.00

**Cerkev Sv Jakob** (St James's Church) Gornji trg 18; tel: 252 1727 [3 D6:D7] **OT**
Services: 08.00, 09.15, 10.30 and 17.00

## *LJUBLJANA CARD*

The Ljubljana Card gives free or reduced entrance into the city's museums, galleries and some special events. It also gives the holder free city bus travel and discounts on guided tours and some souvenirs. Some of Ljubljana's hotels, restaurants, bars and clubs also give tourist card holders a discount, as do some taxi companies, car rental firms and shops. Valid for 72 hours from the time of purchase, the Ljubljana Card is available at TICs and some hotels for 3,000SIT.

**Uršulinska Cerkev Sv Trojice** (Ursuline Church of the Holy Trinity) Slovenska 21; tel: 252 4864 [3 C5] **C**
Services: 08.00, 09.00, 10.00 and 18.00

## TOURIST OFFICES

Located on Stritarjeva, Ljubljana's main tourist information centre (TIC) dishes out free brochures and sells books, sightseeing tours, souvenirs and postcards. The touch screen in the office also has information about Ljubljana and Slovenia (there is a similar screen at the railway station TIC). Both offices can book accommodation in private rooms, apartments, hostels and hotels. The Slovenian Tourist Board also has an information centre in Ljubljana, which has much of the same information and reasonably priced internet access (250SIT for 30 minutes).

Of the wealth of English-language brochures produced by the Ljubljana Tourist Board, the most useful publications are the *Where? Ljubljana Tourist Guide*, which gives an overview of the city's main sights, the *Ljubljana City Map* and *Ljubljana from A to Z*, a tiny directory of addresses and phone numbers. Picking up an annual, monthly or weekly events guide, the glossy *Ljubljana Life* and a copy of the *Slovenia Times* will help you stay on top of social and cultural events.

**Ljubljana Tourist Information Centre** Stritarjeva; tel: 306 1215; fax: 306 1204; email: info@ljubljana-tourism.si; www.ljubljana-tourism.si [3 D5] **C**
Open daily 08.00–21.00 Jun–Sep and 08.00–19.00 Oct–May

**Tourist information centre at the railway station** Trg OF 6, Železniška postaja; tel: 433 9475; fax: 433 0551; email: ticzp@ljubljana-tourism.si; www.ljubljana-tourism.si [1 E5] **C**
Open daily 08.00–22.00 Jun–Sep and 08.00–19.00 Oct–May

**Slovenian Tourist Information Centre** Krekov trg 10; tel: 306 4575; 306 4576; fax: 306 4580; email: stic@ljubljana-tourism.si; www.slovenia-tourism.si [3 E5] **OT**
Open daily 08.00–21.00 Jun–Sep and 08.00–19.00 Oct–May

## LOCAL TOUR OPERATORS

A range of city tours and excursions can be booked at the tourist information centres. Due to the small size of the country most areas of it are accessible on a day trip.

### Walking tours of Ljubljana

Two-hour walking tours of the Old Town and the castle depart from the town hall. The tour price includes a trip on the tourist train. Daily at 10.00 and 18.00 May–September and 11.00 October–April. Price: 1,500SIT; concessions 700SIT.

### Ljubljana by night

This two-hour tour of the Old Town combines a walking tour with a boat trip and finishes with an ice-cream or glass of sparkling wine. Daily 20.30 July–August, 20.00 April–June and September. Price: 2,000SIT.

## Sightseeing tours on request

Two-hour guided walking tours are available in 16 languages and can be booked by groups of 5–50 throughout the year. Price: 8,400–24,000SIT.

## Tourist train to Ljubljana Castle

A daily tourist train runs from Prešernov trg to Ljubljana Castle on the hour: 09.00–21.00 May–September, 10.00–19.00 October–April (weather dependent), 10.00–17.00 November and 11.00–15.00 December. It takes around 15 minutes and return trains leave the castle at 20 minutes past each hour. Price: 600SIT; concessions 400SIT.

## Boat tours

One-hour boat tours depart from the Cankarjevo nabrežje pier during the main tourist season. The boat doesn't travel far, with Trnovo and the Dragon Bridge its extremities, but it makes a change to gečŽŽt this close to the LjubljanicaĪs\. You can pay on board, but might want to book ahead at the TIC during peak season. A candlelit and commentary-less 'Romantic Tour' is also available and includes a glass of sparkling wine. Departure times and frequency change subject to weather and demand so check the timetable pinned on the ship's mast by the pier or at the TIC. Price: 1,500SIT; concessions 700SIT.

## Cycling tours

From May–October the Slovenian Tourist Information Centre runs two-hour guided bike tours for a minimum of three people and a maximum of ten. For insurance reasons only over 16s can go on the tour, which costs 3,000SIT. On Saturdays at 10.00 the bicycle tour is free. Staff at the Krekov trg office can also usually be persuaded to organise off-season tours.

## Further afield

### *General excursions*

The tourist information centres also provide information about and can make bookings for various excursions outside Ljubljana, including Šmarna Gora, the historic town of Škofja Loka, the stunning Vintgar Gorge and the Kamniške Savinje Alps.

**Skok Sport Centre** Marinovseva 8; tel: 512 4402 or 040 218 000; email: info@skok-sport.si; www.skok-sport.si [off map] **OCC**

Located just 7km outside of the city centre on the banks of the Ljubljanica River, the Skok Sport Centre offers kayaking, rafting, mountain biking and beach volleyball. The flexible family team headed by Janez Skok can cater activities to suit all age groups and levels of experience. Rafting on Slovenia's Soča River is a real highlight and costs around 6,240SIT per person. You can also hire rafting, kayaking and mountain bike gear from the centre.

Prices: rafting 3,600–6,240SIT, kayak course (10 hours) 25,000–31,200SIT, mountain bike hire 1,200–14,400SIT (2 hours–1 week).

**Balonarski Center Barje** Flandrova 1; tel: 512 9220, email: balon@siol.net [off map] **OCC**
A unique way to see Ljubljana is from the air aboard a hot-air balloon. This company organises flights out across the Ljubljana marshes with unforgettable views of the city and surrounding mountains.

Kompas and Globtour also offer a variety of excursions from Ljubljana:

**Kompas** Slovenska 36; tel: 200 6222; www.kompas.net [3 C5] **C**
**Globtour** Trg Republike 1; tel: 244 1320; www.globtour.si [3 C5] **C**

4

# Local Transport

Ljubljana is a compact city and the best way to explore it is on foot (see *Walking tour*) or by bicycle.

## AIRPORT TRANSFERS

Public buses leave Brnik Airport for Ljubljana city centre at 05.00 and 06.05 and then on the hour 07.00–20.00 Monday–Friday. At weekends and on holidays they leave at 07.00 and then every two hours 10.00–20.00. Buses travelling from the city centre to the airport leave Ljubljana Bus Station at 05.20 and then at ten minutes past the hour 06.10–20.10 Monday–Friday. At weekends and on holidays they leave at 06.10 and then every two hours 09.10–19.10. Journey time 45 min; one-way fare 740SIT. For more information call the bus station (tel: 090 4230).

Markun (tel: 04 252 1016) operate a private bus/minibus service between the airport and Ljubljana Bus Station. These depart Brnik Airport daily at 07.30, 09.55, 11.30, 13.45, 15.00, 16.00, 18.10, 21.50, 23.00 and midnight. Buses for the airport leave Ljubljana at 05.20, 06.15, 10.25, 12.15, 14.10, 15.30, 17.00 and 22.30. Journey time 30 min; fare 1,000SIT.

There is a taxi rank outside the terminal and the fare to Ljubljana city centre costs around 7,000SIT.

**Ljubljana Brnik Airport** tel: 04 206 1981; fax: 04 206 1109; email: info@lju-airport.si; www.lju-airport.si

## BICYCLE HIRE

Ljubljana is a bike-friendly city, where people of all ages travel by bike and cycle lanes abound. However for the novice fast traffic on the busy main roads and the haphazard approach that other vehicles and pedestrians take towards cyclists, particularly on Prešernov trg and along the banks of the Ljubljanica, can be a little unnerving. From May–October tourists can hire bicycles free of charge as part of the Ljubljana Bike (*Ljubljansko kolo*) scheme. Present your photo ID and a refundable deposit of 1,000SIT at one of the hire locations – Prešernov trg, Plečnikov trg or Trg Osvobodilne fronte (outside the railway station) – and you can take away a single-speed bike. The tourist office at Krekov trg also has bikes available and can usually be persuaded to hire these out year-round. More serious cyclists might want to hire a bike from one of the city's commercial outlets where rates are generally upwards of 200SIT an hour and 500SIT a day. Many hotels also offer bicycle hire to guests.

**E Tours** Kongresni trg 13; tel: 426 9441 [3 C5] **C**
**Café Maček** Krojaška 5; tel: 425 3791 [3 D5] **OT**

## BUS SERVICES

Unless you are staying outside of the city centre, or going on an excursion, there is little need to catch a bus in Ljubljana, as its core is compact and even the suburbs of Krakovo and Trnovo are within easy walking distance. However there is a good local bus service run by LPP (*Ljubljanski Potniški Promet*). There are 21 bus routes in total with the majority running 05.00–22.30, although buses 2, 6 and 11 operate from 03.15 until midnight. Frequency of services is about every 15 minutes, and most bus stops have clearly displayed timetables for you to check. If you pay on boarding there is a flat charge of 300SIT. For those planning on making several journeys plastic tokens (*žetoni*), available from post offices, newsstands, tobacco kiosks and some stores, for 190SIT are better value – look out for the green '*žetoni*' signs. Tokens and daily or weekly passes can also be purchased at the bus station or directly from LPP at the locations listed below. Children under four years old travel free, while those aged between four and ten years pay 50% of the fare. Ljubljana city maps distributed by the tourist information centres have a useful and easy-to-follow metro-style map of the city's bus network on the back.

National and international bus journeys start and terminate at Ljubljana Bus Station (*avtobusna postaja*), which is located on the northern edge of the city centre next to the railway station. It is possible to travel almost anywhere you want to go in Slovenia by bus from Ljubljana, although the frequency of services varies. You can just turn up and pay as you board the bus or make an advance reservation for 120SIT.

**LPP Information Centre** Celovška 160; tel: 582 2420/421/422; email: mail@lpp.si; www.lpp.si (also lost and found) [off map] **OCC**

**LPP Information Centre** Trdinova 3; tel: 434 3248/249 [1 D3] **C**

**LPP Kiosk** Slovenska 55 [1 D3] **C**

**Avtobusna Postaja** Trg Osvobodilne fronte 4; tel: 090 4230; email: avtobusna.postaja@ap-ljubljana.si; www.ap-ljubljana.si. Open 05.30–21.00 [1 E2] **C**

## TAXI

Ljubljana has a wealth of taxis that can be hailed on the street, pre-booked or caught at a taxi rank – these are located near the TIC on Stritarjeva, outside the Slon Hotel on Slovenska, at the railway station and near Mestni trg. At night you will also find taxis parked on Prešernov trg. Taxis are metered, the flagfall is 150SIT and, depending on the taxi company, time of day and method of booking, the per-km rate should be 120–300SIT. Fares for journeys over 30km can usually be negotiated in advance. Dialling 9700, 9701, 9702, 9703, 9704, 9707 and 9709 will connect you to one of six taxi firms.

## RAIL

Ljubljana's railway station (Železniška Postaja Ljubljana) is served by domestic and international services. There is a limited local route, which includes services north to Ježica, Črnuče and Vižmarje, east to Polje and southeast to Rakovnik.

**Železniška Postaja** Trg Osvobodilne fronte 6; tel: 291 3332; email: info@slo-zeleznice.si; www.slo-zeleznice.si [1 E2] **C**

## CAR

A good public transport system, affordable taxis and a compact city centre mean that most visitors have little reason to drive in the city centre. If you are going to bring your own car or hire one then it is useful to book a hotel that offers parking, as competition for the limited number of public spaces is tough and the authorities take parking violations seriously. On-street parking generally costs from 100SIT an hour and you need to check the regulations carefully. Centrally located car parks at Kongresni trg, Krekov trg, Trg Republike, Hotel Turist and Petkovškovo nabrežje are open 24 hours and charge 200–250SIT an hour.

For those thinking about taking day trips from Ljubljana, Slovenia has a comprehensive road network and is easy to explore by car. Driving also provides access to Slovenia's more remote villages and dramatic rural scenery.

## Rules of the road

Traffic in Slovenia drives on the right. Mandatory speed limits are 130km/h on motorways, 100km/h on main highways, 90km/h on regional roads outside residential areas and 50km/h in built up areas. You will often see signs for 70km/h, 60km/h and even 40km/h – these are usually on very winding sections of road, or when workmen are at the side of the road. Many Slovenes do not stick to the speed limits, but you should as the police are vigilant and issue fines and penalty points to speeding drivers. It is illegal to overtake a school bus, seat belt use is compulsory and dipped headlights should be kept on at all times whilst driving. The latter is a fairly new law, so the police may just remind drivers to turn their lights on; however they can issue a fine. The legal alcohol blood level is 0.05% or 0.5g/kg, but it is much safer to avoid alcohol when driving.

For more information on driving in Slovenia contact Auto-Moto Zveza Slovenjie (AMZS) whose emergency roadside number is 1987.

**Auto-Moto Zveza Slovenjie (AMZS)** Dunajska 128; tel: 061 530 5300; fax: 01 568 5317; www.amzs.si. [off map] **OCC**

## Car hire

Car hire costs from around 48,000SIT per week for a budget model and a litre of unleaded petrol costs 190–200 SIT. To hire a car you must be over 21 years old and have held a clean driving licence for at least a year. You also need your national driving licence, passport and a valid credit card. Those under 25 have to pay additional insurance premiums of around 1,200SIT a day. Car hire is available at the airport, in central Ljubljana and at some of the city's hotels.

### *Airport*

**Avis** Tel: 04 236 5000; fax: 04 236 5001; email: lju@avis.si; www.avis-alpe.si. Open 08.00–22.00

**Budget** Tel: 04 201 4300; fax: 04 201 4301; email: budget.car@siol.net; www.budget-slovenia.com. Open 07.00–23.00

**Europcar** Tel: 04 206 1684; email: infoabc@siol.net; www.europcar.si. Open 07.00–21.00

**Hertz** Tel: 04 201 6999; email: info@hertz.si; www.hertz.si. Open 08.00–20.00

**National Car Rental** Tel: 04 238 1020; email: national@avantcar.si; www.nationalcar-slovenia.com. Open 08.00–22.00

**Sixt-Alcom** Tel: 04 234 4666; email: alcom2@siol.net; www.alcom-lj.si. Open 08.00–22.00

### *City centre*

**Avis** Čufarjeva 2; tel: 430 8010; fax: 430 8014; email: lji@avis.si; www.avis-alpe.si. Open Mon–Fri 07.00–19.00, Sat 07.00–13.00, Sun 08.00–12.00 [1 E3] **C**

**Avis** Hotel Lev, Vošnjakova 1; tel: 438 3250; fax: 438 3255; email: lj3@avis.si; www.avis-alpe.si. Open 08.00–15.00 [1 C3] **C**

**Budget** Grand Hotel Union, Miklošičeva 3; tel: 421 7340; fax: 421 7344; email: budget.car@siol.net. Open Mon–Fri 08.00–16.00, Sat and Sun 08.00–12.00 [1 D4] **C**

**Europcar** Hotel City Turist, Dalmatinova 15; tel: 507 6127; fax: 519 9876. Open Mon–Fri 08.00–16.00, Sat 08.00–11.00 and 18.00–20.00, Sun 08.00–11.00 [1 D4:E4] **C**

**Hertz** Avtobusna postaja Ljubljana, Trg Osvobodilne fronte 5; tel: 234 4646; fax: 234 4647; email: info@hertz.si; www.hertz.si. Open Mon–Fri 07.00–19.00, Sat 08.00–13.00, Sun 08.00–12.00 [1 E2] **C**

5

# Accommodation

For a European capital city Ljubljana has a surprisingly small number of hotels. Before Slovenian independence in 1991 there was not really a significant level of demand for accommodation as the city was not a major political, tourist or business destination. Things are starting to improve, although new hotel developments have been slow to take off the ground. Big international chains like Holiday Inn and Intercontinental came in during the 1990s, but have since moved on. Due to the shortage of rooms rates tend to be on the high side when compared to other new European Union members, especially at the most centrally located properties. The opening of two new hotels in 2004, the Domina Grand Media and the Mons Hotel, have helped increase capacity and more plans have been mooted for future developments. Higher-end properties often quote their price in euros, though all prices here are given in tolars and you can often pay in either currency.

Despite capacity problems there is enough accommodation to cater for all tastes and budgets, from the luxurious five-star Lev and a handful of four-star business hotels, through to the basic one-star Bit Center and private pensions. Breakfast is usually included in hotel rates and the availability of triple and even quadruple rooms helps spread the cost. For those travelling on a tighter budget Ljubljana has two year-round hostels, Celica and the Ljubljana Youth Hostel. From June to August some student dorms are transformed into additional hostel accommodation (www.youth-hostel.si). Staff at the tourist information centres will help you book accommodation in pensions and private rooms, which are cost effective at 3,500–5,200SIT per person, but availability can be a problem and some places are situated quite far out of the city centre. A number of private apartments, which are generally charged for at a daily rate are also available.

Regardless of your budget booking ahead is advisable; this is especially true for those looking to snap up a cheaper room.

## CITY CENTRE

**Celica Hostel** (29 rooms) Metelkova 9; tel: 430 1890; fax: 430 1890; email: info@souhostel.si; www.souhostel.si [2 G3] **C**

Just 5 minutes' walk from the bus and train stations, this bright and funky hostel offers 92 beds in 2-, 3-, 4-, 5-, 7- and 14-person rooms, and is one of the most colourful places to stay in Ljubljana. Housed in a former prison that also once served as the military barracks of the Yugoslav army, the best rooms are the 20 renovated prison cells that sleep two or three people. Each of these individual and local-artist-designed cells retains its original window and cell bars, but the bright décor stops them feeling claustrophobic and all of today's inmates are furnished with the luxury of a key to the door. If you stay in a cell then bathroom facilities are shared, but the hostel's 9 other rooms have private bathrooms. Celica also has a room for disabled guests on the ground floor, a bar, café, gallery, internet access, prayer room and a self-service laundry and kitchen. The neighbouring entertainment complex in the Metelkova squat and regular Tuesday evening jam sessions add to the hostel's appeal. Celica's unique style and cheap prices mean that it is often full, so it is essential to book in advance.

From Celica it is a 15-minute walk to the city centre. Per person rates for the under 35s range from 3,500–5,250SIT. For over 35s this increases to 4,950–5,750SIT.

**City Hotel Turist** (123 rooms) Dalmatinova 15; tel: 234 9130; fax: 234 9140; email: info@hotelturist.si; www.hotelturist.si [1 D4:E4] **C**
This centrally located 3-star business hotel is a good option with friendly and helpful staff. All rooms have AC and en-suite bathrooms with showers, desks, alarm clocks and hairdryers. On-street parking, half- and full-board rates and bicycle hire (for guests only) are also available. The hotel also has its own restaurant, bar, soft drinks dispenser and public internet terminals in the lobby. Singles 13,680–22,320SIT, doubles 23,760–33,360SIT, triples 28,320–36,000SIT, business suite 30,240–37,920SIT.

**Grand Hotel Union Business** (139 rooms) Miklošičeva 3; tel: 308 1170; fax: 308 1914; email: hotel.business@gh-union.si; www.gh-union.si [1 D4] **C**
Formerly a Holiday Inn, the modern wing of the Grand Hotel Union has an unattractive exterior compared to its illustrious relation next door. However, guest rooms are furnished to the same high standards as rooms in the Executive and guests have access to all of the facilities detailed in the listing below. There is a modest gym and a small swimming pool that offers sweeping views of the skyline. Singles 32,400–44,800SIT, doubles 42,200–54,000SIT.

**Grand Hotel Union Executive** (191 rooms) Miklošičeva 1; tel: 308 1270; fax: 308 1015; email: hotel.union@gh-union.si; www.gh-union.si [1 D4] **C**
Housed in a stunning art-nouveau building dating from 1905, this is Ljubljana's most attractive hotel and the choice of many visiting celebrities and various movers and shakers, including

George Bush Snr and Bill Clinton. This luxury bolthole is just a minute's stroll from Prešernov trg and the river, as well as the main entertainment area. Classically decorated rooms feature satellite TV, minibars and, that Ljubljana rarity, fluffy bathrobes and slippers. Meeting and conference facilities, good-quality restaurants and garage parking are also on offer. Try to get a room facing out on to Miklošičeva and on one of the higher floors for unique perspectives of the street's stunning art-nouveau treasures and the castle lurking behind. Executive guests can also use the leisure facilities at its Business sibling. The only downside is that this hotel is often full. Singles 32,400–44,800SIT, doubles 42,200–54,000SIT.

**Grand Union Hotel Garni** (74 rooms) Miklošičeva 9; tel: 308 4300; fax: 230 1181 [1 D4] **C**
Renovated in 1999, this centrally located hotel was taken over by the Grand Union in 2004 and attracts a largely business crowd. Service is professional rather than friendly. Large modern guestrooms are comfortable and equipped with all the amenities that you would expect to find in a 4-star hotel including satellite TVs, minibars, in-room internet connections, AC and safety deposit boxes. The hotel also has its own restaurant, bar, relaxation centre with sauna and conference facilities and a hard-to-beat location, just minutes' walk from the main bus and railway stations and 500m from the Old Town. Singles 25,600–28,000SIT, doubles 33,600SIT.

**Lev** (189 rooms) Vošnjakova 1; tel: 433 2155; fax: 230 2578; email: info@hotel-lev.si; www.hotel-lev.si [1 C3] **C**
This is Ljubljana's only 5-star hotel, a place firmly geared towards business people, though there are often good deals at weekends to attract leisure travellers as well. Rooms are

spacious, classically styled and comfortable. En-suite bathrooms have a shower and bath. Standard room facilities include a minibar, satellite and pay TV, AC, writing desk and a small table. The Lev may not be as luxurious as many 5-star hotels around the world, however it lays a fair claim to offering the best accommodation in the city. The hotel also has rooms for disabled guests, a restaurant, bar, small gym, internet point and a beauty parlour. Some of the city-side rooms on the higher levels have castle views and others overlook Tivoli Park. The breakfast buffet is one of the most generous in the city, though it is not always included in the room rate. Singles 46,600–51,300SIT, doubles 56,000–58,300SIT, suite 69,900SIT.

**Park** (122 rooms) Tabor 9; tel: 433 1306; fax: 433 0546; email: hotel.park@siol.net; www.hotelpark.si [2 G3] **C**
The Park is located 800m from the main bus and railway stations and is one of the few budget hotels in Ljubljana. It is a good alternative for those who cannot get a bed in the nearby Celica hostel. Housed in an uninviting concrete tower block it has clean and basic single and double rooms with en-suite facilities, and as few frills as you would expect. Singles 10,800–11,760SIT, doubles 13,920–15,120SIT.

**Pension Pri Mraku** (30 rooms) Rimska 4; tel: 421 9600; fax: 421 9655; email: daj-dam@daj-dam.si; www.daj-dam.si [3 B6] **C**
This guesthouse has a good location on an attractive street near the Križanke theatre, so if you are here for a concert or for the summer festival this is the place to stay. The signs to the reception take you up an old-fashioned burgundy staircase, the kind of décor you can

expect in this charming old time warp. Despite their old-world feel guestrooms are fairly large and have modern facilities including internet access and cable TV. Singles 13,560–16,800SIT, doubles 21,360–25,200SIT, triples 26,160–28,800SIT, 1–4-person suites 36,000–43,000SIT.

**Slon Best Western Premier** (176 rooms) Slovenska 34; tel: 470 1100; fax: 251 7164; email: sales@hotelslon.com; www.hotelslon.com [1 C4] **C**
The Slon has one of the best locations in the city on Slovenska with shops to one side and the city's historic attractions rambling away on the other, not to mention Tivoli Park, which is only a short walk away. The name means 'Elephant' as Emperor Maximilian was once said to have camped his elephants on the site – a large, garish elephant now welcomes you into the lobby. Friendly and helpful reception staff are amongst the most amenable and switched on in the city. In addition to comfortable air conditioned rooms, the Slon offers internet access in the lobby and a ground-floor deli, café and restaurant. Good rates are often available through the Best Western website. The rather dubious cabaret in the basement is geared towards a certain male business demographic. Singles 20,640–28,320SIT, doubles 28,760–39,840SIT, triples 43,920SIT, suites (1–4 people) 42,720–87,840SIT.

**Tour As** Mala 8; tel: 434 2660; fax: 434 2664; email: info@apartmani.si; www.apartmaji.si [1 E4] **C**
Agency co-ordinating stays in apartments. All properties are fully furnished, have telephones, satellite TV and internet connections. Ensure that you know the exact location of your apartment before booking if you want to avoid long walks or buses into town; a handy map

on the company's website will help you do this. Prices range from 14,290–25,000SIT per day depending on location and the number of people that the apartment will sleep.

**Youth Hostel Ljubljana Tabor** (59 beds) Vidovdanska 7; tel: 234 8840; fax: 234 8855; email: ssljddta1s@guest.arnes.si; www.youth-hostel.si [2 F4] **C**
From late June to late August these centrally located student dorms increase the number of hostel beds available in Ljubljana. The accommodation in single-, twin-, triple- and four-bedded rooms is basic but clean. There is also an onsite café-bar and car park, as well as handball, volleyball and basketball courts. Per person rates 3,600–4,800SIT.

## OUTSIDE CITY CENTRE

**AA Lipa** Celovška 264; tel: 507 4590; fax: 507 4960; email: aa-lipa@siol.net; www.aa-lipa.si [off map] **OCC**
*B1 direction Vižmarje, B15 direction Medvode or B16 direction Gameljne to Dravlje stop*
Located on busy Celovška not far from the M Hotel (about 3km out of town), the AA Lipa offers basic motel-style accommodation in an unappealing tower block. Handy if you are in a hurry to get to the airport, but otherwise there is little, other than the price, to recommend this pension. Singles 8,940SIT, doubles 11,930SIT.

**Bit Center** (37 rooms) Litijska 57; tel: 548 0055; fax: 548 0056; email: hotel@bit-centre.net; www.bit-center.net [off map] **OCC**
*B5 or B9 direction Štepansko naselje or B13 direction Sostro to Emona stop*
On the same site as the Ljubljana Youth Hostel this budget hotel is a step up from

dormitory accommodation. Rooms are basic and small with satellite TV and private bathrooms with shower. Guests get a 50% reduction on the facilities offered at the adjoining sports centre and can use the outdoor pool free of charge in the summer. Singles 6,790SIT, doubles 9,590SIT.

**Dijaški Dom Bežigrad** (70 rooms) Kardeljeva ploščad 28; tel: 534 0061; fax: 534 2864; email: dd.lj-bezigrad@guest.arnes.si [off map] **OCC**
B6 *direction Črnuče,* B8 *direction Ježica or* B21 *direction Beričevo to Mercator stop*
Those struggling to find affordable accommodation in Ljubljana could do worse than turn to the student dormitories in Bežigrad, open in July and August. A total of 240 budget-priced beds are offered in basic student rooms with 1, 2 or 3 beds. Per person rates 2,880–4,320SIT.

**Dijaški Dom Ivana Cankarja** (180 rooms) Poljanska 26; tel: 474 8600; fax: 432 0369; email: dd.lj-ic@guest.arnes.si; www.dic-lj.com [4 H6] **OCC**
B5 *direction Štepansko naselje or* B13 *direction Sostro to Roška stop*
The student dorms are just 10 minutes' walk from central Ljubljana, close to Castle Hill. The largest of the part-time youth hostels has 480 beds in single, double and triple rooms from mid June until the end of August. Again rooms are functional and geared towards their term-time student inhabitants. The residence also has its own parking spaces, as well as a sports stadium with a running track, football pitch and basketball courts. Per person rates 2,640–3,840SIT.

**Dijaški Dom Šiška** (50 beds) Aljaževa 32; tel: 500 7802; fax: 500 7820; email: ddsiska@email.si; www.ddsiska.com [off map] **OCC**

*B1 direction Vižmarje, B3 direction Litostroj, B5 direction Podutik, B8 direction Brod, B15 direction Medvode or B16 direction Gameljne to Stara Cerkev stop*

This pleasant student dormitory, located on a leafy street in the suburb of Šiška to the northeast of the Tivoli Park, opens its doors from the beginning of June through to the end of August. Accommodation takes the form of simply furnished twin rooms. This seasonal hostel also has a TV room, café-bar, currency-exchange facilities and a car park. Per person rates 2,640–3,600SIT.

**Domina Grand Media Ljubljana** (213 rooms) Dunajska 160; tel: 569 1192; fax: 569 1193; email: grandmedia.ljubljana@domina.it; www.dominahotels.it [off map] **OCC**

*B6 direction Črnuče, B8 direction Ježica or B21 direction Beričevo*

Opened in summer 2004, one of Ljubljana's newest hotels claims to be the 'Most Hi-Tech Hotel in the World' and it is every technophile's dream. The construction of the hotel ran into numerous problems due largely to the bold and ambitious design, with the opening delayed repeatedly, though the end result is impressive. Comfortable doubles and junior suites, with a modern and arty feel and idiosyncratic décor, offer broadband internet connections, free email, pay TV and computer games. In many rooms huge plasma TV screens also provide on-screen newspapers, books, films and even virtual sightseeing tours of Ljubljana. Additional facilities include an indoor pool, sauna, gym, casino, restaurants, bars, convention centre, meeting rooms and video conferencing. The only bugbear is that the hotel is located 3km out of the city centre, which means you will need to catch the hotel's shuttle bus, a taxi or municipal bus to and from town. Good rates are often available on the internet. From 19,200SIT.

**Ježica Campsite and Bungalows** Dunajska 270; tel: 568 3913; fax: 568 3912; email: ac.jezica@gpl.si; www.gpl.si [off map] **OCC**
*B6 direction Črnuče and B8 direction Ježica to Ježica stop*
Located 3 km from the city centre near the banks of the river Sava, the well-equipped Ježica campsite has electricity points, hot water, showers, laundry and dishwashing facilities, as well as its own recently refurbished restaurant and a snack bar. The 3ha site has the capacity for 300 tents and 600 motor homes. There is the option of renting a bungalow equipped with a telephone and television. Onsite sports facilities include a skittle alley, gym, sauna, games courts and three swimming pools. The campsite reception can give advice about cycling, canoeing, kayaking, tennis, horse riding and fishing (for which they sell licences). Camping 1,730–2,100SIT per person. Bungalows: singles 12,000SIT, doubles 15,000SIT, triples 19,000SIT.

**Ljubljana Youth Hostel** Litijska 57; tel: 548 0055; fax: 548 0056; email: hotel@bit-centre.net; www.yh-ljubljana.com [off map] **OCC**
*B5 or B9 direction Štepansko naselje or B13 direction Sostro to Emona stop*
Affiliated with Hostelling International and providing accommodating in 2-, 3- and 10-bedded rooms. The rooms are bright and modern and guests benefit from a 50% discount on sporting facilities and free usage of the outdoor pool in summer. The hostel also has a car park and a summer terrace bar. Shared bathrooms. Price 2,700SIT per person.

**M Hotel** (157 rooms) Derčeva 4; tel: 513 7000; fax: 519 3048; email: info@m-hotel.si; www.m-hotel.si [off map] **OCC**

*B1 direction Vižmarje, B5 direction Podutik, B8 direction Brod, B15 direction Medvode or B16 direction Gameljne to Šiška stop*

Don't let your first glimpse of the Mercator-owned M Hotel put you off. The hotel is not, as it may at first appear, totally immersed in a jungle of concrete high rises and busy roads. Rooms at the front of the hotel overlook a quiet tree-lined street and Tivoli Park. With friendly staff and modern rooms the M Hotel is a solid 3-star property. The 20–30 minute walk into the city centre may be off-putting, but you can walk part of the way through the park or jump on a bus from Celovška. Now that the raucous Hound Dog club is gone from the basement you have an even better chance of a good night's sleep. Singles 13,450–18,800SIT, doubles 19,588–23,600SIT, extra bed 47,200SIT, suite 38,940SIT.

**Mons Hotel** (114 rooms) Pot za Brdom 55; tel: 470 2700; email: info@hotel.mons.si; www.hotel.mons.si [off map] **OCC**

Opened in September 2004, this stylish design hotel – a box-like green-and-glass structure – is Ljubljana's newest accommodation. Rooms are comfortable and high tech. The hotel also has a wine bar, fitness centre, snooker room, two restaurants and a conference centre making this a perfect hotel for business travellers. For leisure guests however, this new hotel is yet another out-of-town establishment, necessitating a taxi journey to get out there. The hotel does run a free shuttle bus to Kongresni trg. Singles 18,950–23,800SIT, doubles 25,500–29,950SIT, suites 35,950–52,800SIT.

**Vila Minka** Kogovškova 10; tel: 583 0080; fax: 507 4691; email: minka@vilaminka.si; www.vilaminka.si [off map] **OCC**

*B5 direction Podutik or B22 direction Kamna Gorica stop Koseze*

Located 3km from the city centre in the suburb of Koseze just north of Krajinski Park Vila Minka has spacious rooms and apartments. Facilities include satellite TV, internet access and car parking. Apartments also have small private kitchen, while those staying in single or double rooms can use the communal cooking area. Car and bicycle hire is also offered. Singles 10,000SIT, doubles 13,000SIT, apartments 17,000–30,000SIT (1–6 people). A surcharge of 10–30% is applied for stays of less than three days.

# Eating and Drinking

6

Forget any anachronistic images that you may harbour of communist-era culinary deprivations as Ljubljana is fast developing into something of an eating and drinking oasis, a compact city where a smorgasbord of bars, cafés and restaurants are booming. Located on the crossroads between so many European countries it is difficult to say exactly what constitutes definitive Slovenian cuisine: is it the cream-smothered Viennese-style Ljubljana schnitzel, the plump cheese-stuffed Balkan pastry *burek*, spicy Prekmurje goulash or maybe even a bountiful seafood platter caught the same day down on the Adriatic coast and grilled with olive oil and garlic? The truth is that they are all examples of a national cuisine that wholeheartedly embraces Austrian, Hungarian, Croatian and Italian influences, then tops them all off with a generous smattering of genuine Slovenian hospitality.

One constant in Ljubljana's restaurants is the quality of the ingredients; fresh produce is paramount and the daily specials that are recommended by waiters are usually the preferred option of local diners. This is a country where the 'slow food' movement and organic food reign supreme, and where sitting down to a good meal is regarded as a God-given right rather than a luxury. Venues are very loosely divided between *gostilnas*, *gostiščes* and *restavracijas*. In practice these definitions are very blurred, but generally a *gostilna* is an inn that serves drinks and traditional food. The *gostišče* is very similar and also specialises in Slovenian-style dishes, while a *restavracija* tends to be a more formal set-up that may have a more innovative, modern or international menu. In recent years it has become quite trendy to call your new restaurant a *gostilna* or *gostišče* as diners are seeking to re-explore traditional food, further blurring the lines. One constant is a lack of formality and there are few places in Ljubljana that you will feel out of place without a jacket and tie. Handily almost all eating venues have English-language menus and multi-lingual staff.

Over the last few years a number of more exotic cuisines have been sneaking into the Slovenian capital with the likes of Mexican, Japanese and Chinese all now in the mix. In the days before independence in 1991 tucking into a bowl of sushi would have been unimaginable, but today the city's first sushi restaurant is one of Ljubljana's most fashionable spots. The most established 'foreign' cuisine is Italian, with pizza a staple of many Slovenian diets, and the city's myriad pizzerias offer excellent pizza that would not be out of place in Naples.

The day for most locals starts with a light breakfast, increasingly taken on the move with a quick coffee and pastry. Lunch is usually quite a low-key affair except on weekends when it can go on all afternoon and even extend into the evening, especially if you are at a *gostilna* or *gostišče* out in the countryside. Dinner is the main meal of the day and if you are meeting friends you should not plan to do much else afterwards. Slovenes like to take their time over dinner and snake their way through a large number of courses, so if you are lucky enough to snare an invite to dine with some of the *Ljubljančani* settle in for a long haul and remember to wish all of your dining companions '*dober tek*' (*bon appétit*).

Ljubljana offers exceptionally good value when it comes to eating out, though prices do vary markedly from the cheap and cheerful places through to the increasing array of top-end options. Here we have divided venues between top end, mid range, budget, other national cuisines, pizza and fast food, with plenty of choice in each category. Most of Ljubljana's restaurants tend to open for lunch at around noon and stay open until 23.00 or 24.00 Monday–Saturday, with some opening an hour later on Sundays. Restaurants that open for breakfast generally welcome customers from 08.00 and also stay open through to 23.00 or 24.00, while pizzerias often open at 10.00.

## PRICE

### Food

You can pick up a pastry and a hot drink for around 700SIT. In terms of price there is little to differentiate lunch and dinner when ordering à la carte, but a growing number of cafés and restaurants offer fixed-price menus that start at around 1,200SIT and rarely sneak above 4,000SIT. The price guidelines below are for a three-course evening meal excluding wine.

Top end – over 6,000SIT
Mid range – 2,000–6,000SIT
Budget – under 2,000SIT

## Drinks

Soft drinks, mineral water and beer (both on draught and in bottles) come in at around 350–450SIT per drink, while tea and coffee is generally a little cheaper at 250–300SIT. A 10cl glass of wine starts at around 300–400SIT per measure, although in practice most wine drinkers order double measures. If you order a bottle of wine in one of Ljubljana's bars or restaurants this will usually cost upwards of 3,000SIT.

# RESTAURANTS

## Top-end dining

**As Gostilna** Čopova 5a; tel: 425 8822 [1 C4] **C**

Tucked away in a hidden courtyard just yards away from the main action on Prešernov trg is a restaurant that has been up there with the city's best for a few years now. This is the place for a meal amongst Ljubljana's cognoscenti with top-quality cuisine and fine wine, but make sure to dress up smart. The main building has an old-world atmosphere with candles and oil paintings, making it the perfect venue for impressing that special companion. Unusually for Ljubljana you may feel more comfortable in here with a jacket and tie. The outdoor covered terrace has more of a buzz and is less formal. Both venues concentrate on excellent seafood with a shared Adriatic platter to die for, as well as some creative options presented with lashings of flair. The wine list is also excellent and service is seamless. Smooth waiters usually try to coax you into ordering a different glass of wine to accompany each course and if you have the cash you would be well advised to follow their advice.

**Chez Eric** Mestni trg 3; tel: 251 2839; www.delices.si [3 D5] **OT**
For sheer class and top-end French cuisine Chez Eric is hard to beat. The decadent interior and professional waiting staff ensure a quality experience and the food does not disappoint. A flurry of six oysters to start is a popular option or perhaps some *foie gras*? The mains feature the likes of veal medallions and beef tornadoes, while *crêpe suzette* awaits to finish things off, before you are caressed reluctantly back outside into reality.

**Pri Sv Florijanu** Gornji trg 20; tel: 251 2214 [3 E7] **OT**
One of Ljubljana's oldest upscale restaurants has recently been revamped and its intimate and rustic interior has taken on a new chic edge. The menu upstairs expertly fuses Slovenian and French cuisine, making this a great venue for a special occasion with treats like steak laced with a truffle and cream sauce and wrapped in *pršut* or sea bass infused with celery and caviar. Downstairs is a much cosier space called Moro that serves a rich Moroccan menu in suitably Arabic surrounds with a shisha pipe also on hand for that touch of Arab authenticity. There is a large secluded table down here, which is a great option for a group of 10–12. The 1,890SIT lunch and 2,700SIT menus are a complete steal.

**Pri Vitezu** Breg 20; tel: 426 6058 [3 D6] **KT**
This fashionable and classy riverside brasserie and wine bar fuses Italian and Slovenian cuisine, and is a great place to try more adventurous fish dishes and Slovenian roast meats. Do not be afraid to ask the waiting staff for help as the English translation of the dishes does not always do the chef justice. The old-world décor with oil paintings and vaulted

wooden ceilings conjures up the traditional cosiness of the Karst region in the south of the country, making it a great favourite for locals looking to take someone out for a traditional treat. Many diners start with a glass of Slovenian bubbly, guaranteed to get you in the mood for the culinary delights to come.

**Smrekarjev Hram** Nazorjeva 2; tel: 251 6810 [1 D4] **C**
The signature restaurant at the Grand Union Hotel has been at the top of the tree for years, but these days it has a decent set of rivals. With an ambience and appearance more reminiscent of a grand 1920s ocean liner than a Ljubljana hotel, Smrekarjev Hram still delivers on the plate with the likes of pasta with truffles or *pršut* ham to start and grilled sole or venison with marasca cherries amongst the mains. If you fancy a leg of veal (4,200SIT) or leg of lamb (2,500SIT) then you can secure one with a minimum of two days notice. Desserts include that delicious Prekmurje staple: *gibanica*.

**Špajza** Gornji trg 28; tel: 425 3094 [3 E7] **OT**
Špajza reopened following a change of management and refurbishment in summer 2004, but already it is back to its best. This is the archetypal Slovenian upmarket restaurant, managing to conjure up first-class cooking, fresh ingredients and a cosy, informal ambience where jeans are

perfectly acceptable. In season (autumn) opt for Istrian truffles (*tartufi*) which come served simply with pasta and cream as a starter or taking beef fillet and monkfish to new levels as a main. At other times consider opting for sea bass if it is the fish of the day as the whole fish is cooked to perfection and is more than a meal for two. The wine list is reasonable value, but Špajza is definitely a candidate for the most expensive restaurant in the city.

## Mid range

**Figovec** Gosposvetska 1; tel: 446 4210 [1 C3] **C**

One of the oldest coaching inns in the city serves up a menu that will have vegetarians diving for cover. Horse meat comes in various permutations and there are the likes of pigs' trotters for the adventurous. More mainstream Slovenian dishes include grilled Adriatic squid and Prekmurje-style goulash. The décor just about steers on the right side of tacky with hanging lamps, farmyard tools, black-and-white photos and wooden beams.

**Gostilna Sokol** Ciril Metodov trg 18; tel: 439 6855; www.gostilna-sokol.com [3 D5] **OT**

A bustlingly popular *gostilna* close to the central market serving lashings of hearty traditional food including goulash, wild boar, Slovenian blood sausage and chunky vegetable broth, all washed down by generous carafes of wine. If you like your meat then this is the place to head, but vegetarians and those on a diet would be well advised to steer clear. Sokol buzzes at lunchtime when the market is on and is good at New Year when there is live music and a traditional feast – bookings essential. A good choice for those in a group or on stag and hen weekends as they are happy to cater for groups.

**Julija** Stari trg; tel: 425 6463 [3 D6] **OT**
The perfect venue for an unrequited love affair as it is named after the girl that Slovenia's national poet, France Prešeren, fell hopelessly in love with. The restaurant itself was refurbished a few years ago with an informal feel and equally informal menu that ventures across the border into Italy more than once with the likes of *carpaccio* or *caprese* salad to start and pasta or risotto to follow. In summer there are tables out on busy Stari trg.

**Operna Klet** Župančičeva 2; tel: 252 7003 [1 B4] **C**
Hiding away by the opera house in a small cellar is one of Ljubljana's best seafood restaurants. The dark wood fish swimming across the old stone walls and hardwood panelling make Operna Klet easy on the eye, but you will soon be concentrating on the plate with the likes of crab croquettes and tartar sauce and grilled squid with garlic to start. Grilled fresh fish is the highlight of the main menu. In summer there is also an outdoor terrace upstairs.

**Pen Club** Tomsičeva 12; tel: 251 4160 [1 B4] **C**
Traditionally the meeting place for the Slovene literati, this intimate venue has a menu that changes daily. With décor that has a discernible 1970s edge the Pen Club manages to be pleasingly kitsch without even trying. There are no English menus, but the staff are more than happy to explain a menu that includes starters such as pasta laced with white truffles or homemade ravioli stuffed with spinach. The fish dishes are the stand outs amongst the mains with fresh fish brought for inspection before cooking, with huge sea bass – usually more than enough for two – a speciality. Lunch can be a quite subdued affair in this quiet embassy district,

while dinner attracts enough movers and shakers to make eavesdropping all part of the fun. Reservations essential for dinner.

**Rusalka** Vosnjakova 1; tel: 433 2155 [1 C3] **C**
The Lev hotel's ground-floor restaurant styles itself as 'international', but the highlights are often the excellent Slovenian dishes. The venison with cracked pepper and cranberries is melt-in-the-mouth sublime, though the dandelion (yes, really) salad takes a bit of getting used to, as well as a lot of chewing. Regular promotions bring in the likes of sushi to a hotel restaurant that goes against the grain and is actually worth visiting even if you are not staying here. The dining space is light and simple with window tables where you can sit and watch the street outside, while staff are not too stuffy, making this an ideal venue for a relaxed lunch.

**Vinoteka** Dunajska 18; tel: 431 5015; www.vinoteka-bradesko.si [1 D1] **OCC**
The days when all of the big Yugoslav fairs and exhibitions kept Vinoteka busy are long gone and it has now settled into a comfortable and more sedate middle age. The rustic décor features solid wood tables and snugs that were fittingly made from wine barrels. Wine may be the *raison d'être* of Vinoteka, but the food stands up well too with platters of *pršut* and Slovenian cheese a perfect accompaniment for a full-bodied *Teran* red from the Karst region, while warm starters like flavoursome wild asparagus are perfect with a glass of white wine from the banks of the Drava. A sturdy *Lisjak Modri Pinot* is a good partner for the wild venison on the main menu and you can finish the feast off with a glass of Slovenian dessert wine. Service is knowledgeable and friendly and if you have enjoyed the wine you can pick up a bottle or two in the shop on the way out. If you are

lucky, wine connoisseur and *bon vivant* owner Simon Bradeško will be on hand to offer a few tips.

**Zlata Ribica** Cankarjevo nabrežje 5; tel: 241 0690 [3 D5] **OT**
This refurbished riverside restaurant in the heart of the Old Town serves a mix of hearty Slovenian meat dishes, Italian-influenced cuisine and vegetarian meals. Its waterside terrace has good views and makes for a pleasant dining space on warmer days. Not as cheap as it was before its revamp, but still reasonable value with the likes of baked sea bass laced with shrimps coming in at around 4,000SIT. The pasta dishes come in standard- and large-size portions, with the latter easily large enough to make a meal in themselves. The wine list is fairly extensive and the amenable waiters are only too happy to run through it with you, though prices are not cheap with a *Malvasija* coming in at over 3,000SIT, an unthinkable price down in the south of the country where it is drunk like water.

## Budget

**Pri Pavli** Stari Trg; tel: 425 9275 [3 D6] **OT**
This plain and simple restaurant in the Old Town serves up dependable traditional cooking. The cold platters to share are meals in themselves with lashings of local cheese and *pršut* ham from the south, along with more exotic offerings that are not for the squeamish like beef testicles. Other more mainstream options include grilled squid, Balkan meat grills and pizza. Service can be a touch surly, especially when they are busy. Set menus are priced at 1,300SIT for lunch or 1,600SIT for dinner.

**Pri Škofu** Rečna 8; tel: 426 4508 [3 C7:D7] **KT**

Fittingly laid back for this part of the city in Krakovo, Pri Škofu recently reopened and is now satisfying local students as well as visitors willing to wander slightly off the main tourist route. There is no menu as such with bright, young waitresses gaily recanting the day's offerings, usually a choice of soup to start, including a heart-pumping ginger concoction, before a main course of seafood risotto, roasted turkey or the house speciality, plump beef steak cooked with a peppercorn crust. Do not be put off by the tiny bar at the entrance as the main smoking and non-smoking restaurant sections are inside to the right. Very Ljubljana and very popular.

**Ribca** Tržnica Jožeta Plečnika [3 D5] **OT**

For budget seafood Ribca is hard to beat. Located beneath Plečnik's colonnades just by the fish market the seafood could not be much fresher or better value. The no-frills menu features the likes of grilled squid and shrimp, anchovies and hake. If you are struggling to understand the menu – few of the waiting staff here speak English – then just spy across at your fellow diners for help. The terrace is pretty no frills with plastic chairs, but there are views out over the river and back towards Prešernov trg. All part of the fun is watching the tourists, who cannot work out a way of getting down to join you, flock over the bridge above. Take the steps that descend down from the shops beneath the colonnades.

**Šestica** Slovenska 40; tel: 242 0850 [1 C4] **C**

Huge portions and cheap prices have punters still piling into one of the city's oldest *gostilnas* after all these years. The building dates to 1670 with the first inn on the site opened in 1776. Back then it was at number six (hence the name) and these days it is on the map thanks to its hearty soups, spicy goulash and chunky risotto. The service can be a little cursory, but for a cheap and filling meal Šestica usually fits the bill.

**Tomato** Šubičeva 1; tel: 252 7555 [3 C5] **C**
Fresh and healthy food is on offer at this massively popular take-away and restaurant. Tomato make sandwiches for many of the city's cafés and it is easy to see why with fresh, inventive toppings and generous portions. There are over 30 sandwich permutations and there is also plenty of scope for choosing your own. Their fresh juices and pastries are an ideal breakfast option especially when the sun is shining as they have seating outdoors. Inside there is also a decent amount of seated space, providing respite when the showers sweep in. A popular place especially with local students so it always has a bit of a buzz.

**Vegedrom** Vodnikova 35; tel: 519 3901 [off map] **OCC**
Just northwest of Cesta na Bellevue the road becomes Vodnikova, where you will find Ljubljana's only vegetarian restaurant. A real gem, this homely oasis serves tempting soups, sandwiches, vegetarian plates for two, tofu, gnocchi and risotto. Equally tempting are desserts like *gibanica* – the traditional Prekmurje pastry cake. If you have been struggling to eat your five daily portions of fruit and vegetables, there is also a self-service salad bar. This relaxed retreat is the perfect venue for a healthy lunch before a stroll in nearby Tivoli Park.

## Other national cuisines (all mid range)

**Cantina Restaurantes Mexicana** Knaflev prehod; tel: 426 9325 [3 D5] **C**
Ousting a busy bar from this central location may not have been a popular move, but the

Cantina is trying to make amends by offering passable *fajitas* and *burritos* in pleasant surrounds. The candlelit terrace is the place to be in summer, while the well-thought-out interior also looks the part. The one downside is the service as it can take an eternity to get noticed, never mind place an order.

**Okrepčevapnica** Vrtna 8; tel: 041 843106 [3 D7] **KT**
'Welcome to Sarajevo' reads the sign as you enter and this new grill restaurant really does offer a slice of Bosnia in a thoughtfully refurbished house in Krakovo. The simple menu offers *čevapčiči* (meat balls), *pleskavica* (meat pattie) and *sudukice* (thin sausages), which come served with fluffy Balkan bread, crispy onions and creamy *kajmak* cheese. Okrepčevapnica's décor is themed without being tacky with old photos of Sarajevo, football strips and Bosnian magazines. The two large communal tables are a nice touch as are the low tables and chairs for families. Another memorable feature are the gloriously politically incorrect Turkish coffees, which come served with a cigarette.

**Sichuan** Gornji trg; tel: 251 9337 [3 E6] **OT**
Ljubljana's first Chinese restaurant is still going strong despite a sprinkling of recent imitators. Anyone expecting the fiery cuisine of the eponymous Chinese region may be disappointed, though, as everything is definitely catered towards more timid local palates with the likes of staples such as black bean soup and sweet and sour chicken. Still, for anyone hankering for a bit of Chinese in an Old Town location Sichuan is a decent option. Outdoor tables in summer.

**Sushimama** Wolfova 12; tel: 426 9125 [3 D5] **C**

Styling itself as 'modern Japanese cooking', this funky central restaurant is the first in the city to serve up fresh sushi and it does not disappoint. The chic minimalist décor and black-clad waiting staff give Sushimama a hip vibe that has quickly attracted the city's smart set. There are also meat dishes such as beef *teriyaki* on the menu in what has instantly become a hot Ljubljana restaurant. There are booths and tables, but if you are on your own or feeling nosy then take a pew at one of the stools in the window and you can watch all of the action outside on busy Wolfova. They have Japanese beer too, including the excellent Asahi, which goes very well with sushi, though steer clear of the saki if you want to emerge walking in a straight line.

## Pizza

Given its proximity to Italy it is no surprise that pizza is ubiquitous in Ljubljana. Thankfully all thoughts of stuffed-crust and American-style deep-pan pizzas have been eschewed in favour of lighter Italian-style offerings that would often satisfy the most demanding of Neapolitan palates. An option for those in a hurry are the ubiquitous Pizza Napoli kiosks (a very popular one is located just along the river from Café Maček), though the quality here is not always the highest. For those on a tight budget Ljubljana's generous pizzas can be a life saver. Ask any local where the best pizza is on sale and you will get a different reply, with the main contenders:

**Čerin** Trubarjeva 52; tel: 232 0990 [2 F4] **OCC**

Very handily located and dependable pizza joint in the city centre. The thin-crust pizzas here are excellent with a base that is not too doughy, but not too hard either. The staff are very flexible with toppings so you can basically design your own, though this does usually entail a longer wait. A bonus is the free internet access that keeps you busy while you wait.

**Foculus** Gregorčičeva 3; tel: 421 9295; www.foculus.com [3 D6] **C**
'Probably the most popular pizzeria in Slovenia' scream the flyers and its large and bustling interior, with its big tables and ceiling paintings, is certainly a bit of a surprise on this sleepy street. The pizza list is extensive with over 50 choices that include all the usual suspects, while at weekends families rule as kids are brought along for a treat. The salad bar is good too as are the desserts. There are tables outside, but be quick as in summer at weekends they are usually snapped up very quickly.

**Ljubljanski Dvor** Dvorni trg 1; tel: 251 6555 [3 D5] **C**
A spacious outdoor terrace, with unrivalled views back across the river to Ljubljana's Old Town, make this restaurant and pizzeria an enduring favourite with visitors and locals alike. Good service and a wide selection of massive wood-fired pizzas (do not even contemplate ordering anything bigger than the gigantic 'classic') and pasta make this a popular choice. The toppings are seemingly endless, though pepperoni with added jalapeño peppers appears to be the local favourite. The back of the restaurant on Kongresni trg serves up take-away pizza and ice-cream, while upstairs is a 'proper' restaurant serving an extensive menu of international dishes. The lunch and set menus here are very good value. Whilst not quite as tasty as dishes ordered from the à la carte menu, a generous 4-course meat- or fish-based menu served at lunchtime costs around 3,500SIT.

**Trta** Grudnovo nabrežje 21; tel: 426 5066 [3 D8] **OT**
This pizzeria is a little further out than the others in the suburb of Prule, opposite Trnovo in an old artistic district of the city by the river. The pizzas here are huge and you may want to ask for two plates and share them with a companion – they come in small and large sizes but both are huge. The fresh mushroom pizza here is divine as is the seafood special with shellfish, langoustines and roe. The '*dynamit*' pizza lives up to its name with enough chilli to stop a small army. In summer there is a terrace by the river and a smattering of wooden benches around the side, which make a good place to while away a few hours munching and chatting by the water. The interior is quite cosy and homely with wooden beams on the ceiling and chunky wood seats.

## *FOR THAT SPECIAL OCCASION*

When you are …

Looking for a romantic meal for two? As Gostilna (main building) or Špajza.

Strapped for cash? Check out Ribica, Tomato, Ljubljanski Dvor or Nobel *burek* or grab a horse burger from the stand in Tivoli or the take-away on Trubarjeva.

After authentic Slovenian cooking? Make a beeline for Pri Vitezu or Gostilna Sokol.

In search of a healthy fix? Don't miss Tomato or Vegedrom.

## FAST FOOD (all budget)

**Tržnica (Central Market)** [3 E5] **OT**

Down behind Plečnik's colonnades the sprawling market offers a range of affordable culinary goodies every day bar Sunday. There are vans dispensing fresh Adriatic seafood as well as a network of stalls offering fresh fruit and vegetables. Small producers also sell ornately bottled honey and pear brandy from Pleterje Monastery, the latter with a full-sized pear inside the bottle, both of which make great souvenirs. This traditional set-up is, for the moment at least, a refreshing world away from supermarket hegemony and EU directives. Amidst the colonnades is a sprinkling of more permanent shops that sell excellent bread, meats, pastries and *burek*.

### *Hot Horse*

Just as it sounds, this particular local 'treat' consists of a huge burger bun stuffed with horse meat, various relishes and vegetables. Ljubljana's late-night drinking set insist you have not been on a real night out until you have topped it off with a horse burger from the stand at the northern side of Tivoli Park [1 A2:B2] **OCC** across from the Lev Hotel. The Hot Horse take-away at Trubarjeva 31 [1 E4] **C** is more central, but for the real authentic experience Tivoli is the place to go. A liberal dose of alcohol in your bloodstream is nigh essential before tackling a horse burger.

### *Burek*

*Burek* may be more of a southern Balkan staple, but amongst local students and workers this instantly filling snack is very popular. It basically consists of a wrap of moist pastry that is stuffed with either meat or soft cheese, with both a worryingly high fat and calorie content. It makes great comfort food though. Arguably the best place to try *burek* is at the central Nobel take-away at Miklošičeva 30 [1 D4] **C**, but as long as it is piping hot and has not been sitting around *burek* is the sort of comfort food that you cannot go too far wrong with.

## CAFÉS/TEA ROOMS AND BARS/WINE BARS

The citizens of Ljubljana like nothing better than settling down in a café or bar for a *bela kava* (milky coffee) or a glass of Union (the local beer). The lines between what constitutes a bar and a café are as blurred as the boundaries between the city's restaurants with coffee often available way into the early hours of the morning in buzzing bars and beer on sale with breakfast in many cafés. Closing times are often the only thing that really differentiate cafés from bars, with the majority of the cafés winding down before midnight during the week, whilst bars generally stay open until 01.00. If you are a night owl there are plenty of late-opening bars that serve drinks until 02.00–03.00. At weekends the key is to start late and build up steadily, with the action not really getting going until after 22.00.

Most cafés and bars tend to be waiter service, though in the Irish and British theme bars you can go to the bar to buy a drink. Getting the attention of a waiter at the height of summer along the riverside can be a nightmarish experience, but a friendly smile and a *dober večer* (good evening) usually helps. Lengthy drink lists adorn most tables, with *kava mjelko* (the closest incarnation to British or American coffee with milk) and *cappuccino* joined by the usual range of soft drinks, though do not expect diet options to be available. Beers normally come in 25cl or 50cl sizes, with the option of having them in the bottle or on *točeno* (draught), though most locals these days seem to prefer bottles. Refreshingly, domestic brands of bottled beer are not noticeably more expensive than those served on draught, though this isn't the case for imported beers, which generally tend to be more expensive.

Like their neighbours across the border in Italy the locals love nothing better than lazing away a few hours on a warm day at an outdoor table, so at the first inkling of warm weather the city's pavements burst to life with a plethora of tables. The emphasis is firmly on people-watching and to fit in just grab a coffee, don your shades and try to look as uninterested as possible while you avidly survey the passing crowds. There is no hurry to move on, and indeed trying to persuade the waiter that you want your bill in anything less than an hour often takes some doing. Occasionally if you are lucky waiting staff will ask you to settle the bill when they bring your drinks – this is simply to make their lives easier during busy periods and is not intended to rush you.

In winter the action moves indoors when mulled wine and a cosy beer are the order of the day.

Ljubljana's café and bar scene these days is increasingly sophisticated. Alongside the old-world cafés and grungy bars are an array of bright new drinking venues, complete with guest DJs, funky décor and waiting staff that would not look out of place in a glossy fashion magazine. New cafés and bars open and close with alarming regularity and the best advice is to tap a local to find out where the newest hip venue of choice is. Here we have tried to split the ever-expanding number of venues into out and out cafés (including tea rooms) and then bars and wine bars.



## Cafés

**Abecedarium Café Cenik** 2 Ribji trg; tel: 426 9514 [3 D5] **OT**

This café claims to be located in the oldest house in the city, which dates back as far as 1528. There is a coat of arms above the door that supposedly relates to one-time mayor of Ljubljana and wine merchant Wolfgang Bosch. It is also said that Primož Trubar, regarded by many as the father of Slovenian literature, also lived here for a while. Today this is a quiet café option just a stone's throw from the river that never seems to get as busy as its nearby rivals. Good choice of coffees and beers and some decent snacks and light meals too.

**Antico** Stari trg 27; tel: 426 5628 [3 D6] **OT**

Less pretentious than many of the new arrivals in this part of town, this relaxed café is an ideal venue for flicking through a guidebook or newspaper. The coffee is the excellent

Illy brand from Trieste and it, along with a couple of chandeliers, helps warm up a dark interior. Wonderfully moist *tiramisu* and a decent choice of Slovenian wines invite a longer stay.

**Bar Grad** Grajska planota 1; tel: 432 7216 [3 E5] **OT**
Not as tacky or as expensive as you might expect for a café in the city's number one tourist attraction. Inside the castle walls, and worth the effort of the walk up on a sunny day, this unpretentious café makes up for a rather dim interior space with a flush of outdoor tables when the weather allows. Friendly and efficient waiting staff and local newlyweds milling around (weddings are conducted here at weekends) make Bar Grad a pleasant place to relax and take in the surrounds of the hotpotch castle architecture. Especially enjoyable on balmy nights when candles are placed on the tables.

**Čajna Hiša** Stari trg 3 [3 D6] **OT**
Ljubljana's first and only dedicated teahouse is doing a roaring trade. Plenty of thought and investment has gone into a set-up that features a relaxed main area with an open second level that retains some of its original painted ceiling. The range of teas is almost endless with no fewer than six different types of green tea and there are also a few coffee and alcoholic options, while a bountiful cake display tempts right in the middle of the café. If you opt for one of the wickedly creamy cakes, then why not top it off with an equally calorific hot chocolate? Off to the right when you enter is a shop selling all sorts of tea, mugs and various tea paraphernalia. The city's supermarkets cannot even begin to match the myriad teas on sale in this charming oasis.

### *STAG AND HEN PARTIES*

These days with the likes of Prague and Amsterdam becoming almost *passé* for stag and hen parties, prospective brides and grooms are casting their nets wider with Ljubljana emerging as an alternative choice. It is easy to see why they come here as there are now budget flights from the UK, Germany and Switzerland, and the city has no shortage of bars, but anyone planning a stag or hen party in the Slovenian capital may want to consider that cheap accommodation is in short supply, most shops close from midday on Saturday until Monday morning, and due to its small size just two or three raucous stag or hen parties can make things feel crowded. Saying that, with friendly English-speaking locals, affordable food and drink and a culture where drinking is socially acceptable, Ljubljana does look set to grow as a stag and hen destination. Also for groups looking to see a bit more than the bottom of a beer glass there are plenty of sightseeing options as well as day trips to the likes of Bled and Bohinj or an adrenaline-filled day out with the likes of Skok Sport (www.skok-



**Kavarna Evropa** Slovenska 47; tel: 438 2400 [1 C3:D3] **C**

While the Kavarna Evropa has lost some of its original charm, when it was part of the luxury Hotel Evropa, and calling it faded may be an understatement, it is still worth visiting for the stab at old-world opulence, not to mention the first-rate coffees. The choice of seating is split between the brighter revamped section and the more atmospheric booths where chandeliers hang above and the echoes are of Paris in the 1920s. The coming of EU membership and Ljubljana's new place in Europe does not seem to have created a flush of business for the Evropa, which has settled into a comfortable middle age. This may soon change as the Luka Gourmet people are said to be about to take over part of the café.

**Kavarna Planet Pločnik** Prešernov trg [3 D5] **C**
When the sun shines this is the place to be in the shadow of the statue of France Prešeren right at the heart of the city by the river. The square bubbles with action day and night and from your vantage point you can take in the mopeds, bikes and bendy buses, along with the ambling pedestrians who somehow manage to share the square with all the other traffic. The sprinkling of tables and chairs wrap around a brightly lit bar, with black-clad staff busy between tables keeping the coffee and stronger drinks flowing. Powerful heat lamps ensure that the people-watching stretches on late into the night with sandwiches on hand so that you do not have to surrender your prized ringside seat. The café also has a small counter by the river selling delicious ice-cream. Another sugary treat is the *kremna rezina*, a deliciously tempting cream cake. In summer there is regular live music right in front of the café.

**Le Petite Café** Trg Francoske Revolucije 4 [3 C6] **KT**
If you are taking in any shows at the Križanke theatre or are attending the Summer Festival this friendly café is the perfect pit stop. It is also handy if you are walking out to

Trnovo and fancy a break on the way. Many of the clientele are students who like nothing better than recreating that Parisian Left Bank feel, which the owners have tried to conjure up with the décor and doors that flip out into the pavement area. The café after all does look out over the only statue of Napoleon Bonaparte outside France. Packed in summer, this is a good place to meet a few locals in an environment that never seems to get too touristy. You can almost forgive the service, which has to be amongst the slowest in the city.

**Luka Gourmet Lunch Café** Stari trg 9 [3 D6] **OT**

Run by the people behind Pri Vitezu here you can sample the same quality ingredients that make the mother restaurant such a success. On sunny days the tables outside are the perfect place to enjoy the ridiculously good-value 1,200SIT set menus, which include soup to start followed by a green salad and a main course which could be prawn and dill pasta, or grilled beef with hand-cut chips and tomato. The à la carte menu offers a salad bar, pasta dishes and a sprinkling of meat and fish options, all cooked freshly with a touch of panache. The wine list is quite limited and they only have Union beer, but this is a great venue for a good-value lunch in the Old Town.

**NUK Café** Turjaška 1 [3 C6] **KT**

While you may not be able to delve into Plečnik's stunning reading rooms you can at least pop down to the café/canteen in the basement that was designed by the great artist himself. Neat lines, funky tables and top-class *bela kavas* are the order of the day and this is a good option for those looking to laze around with local students leafing through a newspaper or trying to strike up a conversation with your guidebook on show. While the library insists on silence no-one frowns on conversation in this relaxed little café.

**Zvezda** Wolfova 14 [3 D5] **C**

Few cafés in Ljubljana can claim to have a better range of cakes and pastries than this sugar-laced wonderland. Forget counting the calories and just fight your way to the counter and indulge. Both the seats on the stylish interior and the outdoor terrace, which overlooks Kongresni trg, are often jam packed so you may well have to take your treat away. If you do get a seat hold on to it, especially on a busy weekend evening. Has a solid claim to having the largest *kremna rezinas* in the city.

## Bars and wine bars

**AS Lounge** Knaflev Prehod 5a [3 C5] **C**

On busy nights this subterranean retreat buzzes with energy as students and the pre-club set work themselves up for a big night. The restaurant above is one of the city's most expensive and formal, but there are no airs and graces about this party venue. When there are live DJs on, the bar area can descend into a throbbing mass of dancing bodies.

**Breg 2** Breg 2 [3 D6] **C**

Pretentious it may be and not very busy even at weekends, but if you like your art and your wine this 'Art and Wine Gallery' is a nigh essential stop. There are various one-off events on here, which to some extent explains why this newcomer has so far failed to really establish a regular clientele. The food is reasonable, but it is the wine you should come for with produce from all the various wine-producing areas of the country.

**Café Galerija** Mestni trg [3 D5] **OT**

One of the city's chicest drinking dens which would not look out of place in a spread for a fashion magazine. Delve through the modest foyer, itself used for various happenings, art exhibitions and catwalk-style shows, and you enter a world of candlelit glamour, awash with mirrors, bountiful sofas and Ottoman décor. The usual beer and wine suspects sit alongside a decent list of cocktails, including a more than passable stab at a Cosmopolitan. If you want to really live it up then this is the place to be, though dress to impress as this is a firm favourite of the local beautiful people and the style police may be on patrol.

**Café Maček** Krojaška 5 [3 D6] **OT**

For years this has been *the* place to be down on the riverside. 'Meet me at Maček' is still an often-heard refrain around the city as everyone always seems to end up here at some point over a weekend. When the weather allows the main action is outside where rampant people-watching and river breezes are perfect company for a cold glass of Union or Laško or a heart-starting *macchiato*. When Maček is too busy in summer just pop next door to Boheme, which has a similar terrace set-up. The often overlooked interior is surprisingly old fashioned and cosy with black-and-white photos on the walls and tables packed around the corner from a British-style bar. Bizarrely Maček also rent out bikes so if you fancy a pedal after your coffee this is the place to come.

**Casa del Papa** Celovška 54; tel: 434 3158 [off map] **OCC**
*B1 direction Vižmarje, B5 direction Podutik, B8 direction Brod, B15 direction Medvode or B16 direction Gameljne*
This multi-level venue has been paying homage to Hemingway for years, but still it has a sparkle. Choose from the Key West pub, the Latino Klub Cuba and the à la carte restaurant. There is much more to Casa del Papa than eating and drinking and it is worth heading out here from the city centre with regular salsa dancing and literary evenings. It is also a good venue for a hearty breakfast, which may help you recover from overindulging on the tempting cocktails the night before. Follow Gosposvetska northwest as it becomes Celovska.

**Cutty Sark** Knaflev prehod 1; tel: 425 8822 [3 C5] **C**
Within easy staggering distance of Prešernov trg, Cutty Sark seems to have a magnetic hold for Ljubljana's expat community. All the home comforts are here in a decent stab at a British bar set-up with a big bar area, bar service available and a range of beers and ales including Guinness and Kilkenny. One of the best things about Cutty Sark is that it is also popular with local students, making it a good place to meet some new Slovene friends, though whether you can hear them amidst the bustle and noise of a busy weekend night here is another matter.

**Fraga** Mestni trg 15 [3 D5] **OT**
This minimalist new bar in the Old Town is bedecked with intriguing modern art and attracts a suitably pretentious, but still friendly, crowd. Sit on the sofas or cram into a funky plastic chair, admire the artwork and enjoy the literary nights and various events. Some of the seats are more stylish than comfortable, unless you get one of the sofas, so you

probably won't stay too long, but Fraga is still well worth popping into for a drink or two as well as information on club nights.

**Guinness Pub** Gosposka 3 [3 C6] **C**
This decent stab at the Irish theme bar concept serves up passable pints of the eponymous Irish stout. The late opening attracts the non-clubbing drinking crowd, though nights tend to end a bit abruptly when they unsubtly switch off the lights to force stragglers out. Beware

### *BEER BATTLES*

The main brewers in Slovenia are Union in Ljubljana and Laško from the eponymous town in the east of the country. Traditionally the *Ljubljančani* have stayed loyal to Union, whose gigantic brewery is unmissable as it stands on the edge of the city centre by Tivoli Park, while Laško has increasingly come to dominate outside of the capital and expanded into other countries in the region, such as Croatia and Montenegro. The picture has been muddied recently with a battle over ownership of Union, which has seen Laško locking horns with international brewery giants Interbrew. After an interminable struggle Laško has taken a 54% stake with Interbrew ending up with 41.3%. This situation is not ideal as it still leaves questions hanging over the future of Union. Worries amongst loyal Union drinkers that the flavour and even the brand may disappear have so far proved unfounded. Both Union and Laško have a variety of tipples to suit all tastes:

marauding British rugby teams who seem to have established this as their Ljubljana HQ on their increasingly frequent visits to the country. At other times this is a handy and welcoming stop off.

**Holidays Pub** Slovenska 36 [1 C4] **C**
This busy little pub is a good stand-by on Slovenska. The cosy British-style pub interior is often a largely male preserve, but the bar staff are friendly and there are leather seats and

***Union*** (www.pivo-union.si)
The main Union product is simply called Union and comes in a trademark red can or bottle. It is backed up by the Union 1964 lager beer, a dark beer (*Črni Baron*) and a pils. A newer product is Smile, a beer with lemon that is very popular with the younger inhabitants of the city and is sold in many clubs and bars. There are tours of the brewery (see *Sightseeing*).

***Laško*** (www.pivo-lasko.si)
Their most famous product is Zlatorog, a refreshing beer which usually comes in 50cl bottles. They also do a dark beer (*Temno*), a low-alcohol beer (*Gren*) and an ever-increasing range of other brews. The newest product is *Roler*, a beer with a twist of lemon to cater for the younger market.

tables where you can dodge the serious drinkers propping up the bar. The drinks choice is decent with Guinness and Kilkenny served on draught and a smattering of fine single malt whiskies. Given the central location and the Best Western hotel next door the pub also attracts a sprinkling of tourists too.

**Kratochwill** Kolodvorska 14; tel: 433 3114 [1 E3] **C**
Now that Katacombe on Stari trg has become the Konoba and no longer produces its own beer Kratochwill stands alone as the city's only micro-brewery pub. The '*Svetlo*' and '*Temno*' (light and dark beers) are available in 20cl, 30cl, 50cl and huge 1-litre glasses, and may not suit all tastes, as they are both decidedly sour and some locals insist the quality has been going downhill in recent years. In summer the terrace is a good place to sit if you are waiting on a train or bus from the central station.

**Makalonca** Hribarjevo nabrežje [3 D5] **C**
In summer this is the place to be down on river level below the crowds milling over the bridge above. Follow the candles down the stairs on the opposite side of the footbridge from where Ljubljana's only tour boat is berthed and you will enter a buzzy bar space. Do not breeze past the bar and take a seat outside as table service is very erratic and it is much easier to grab a drink at the bar. There are two main seating areas, with candlelit outdoor tables the perfect setting for relaxing and congratulating yourself on finding this great spot. Inside the small bar area is perfect for those not enjoying the river breezes. Projections beam across the river and the lights of the Old Town shimmer back in a bar where if you get a coveted riverside table you will want to hog it all night.

**Minimal** Mestni trg 4 [3 D5] **OT**

As minimal as the name suggests the interior is practically polar with white, white and more white. Do not let the beautiful staff and artsy ambience put you off, though, as this is a relaxed venue for a coffee in the afternoon or something stronger at night when the posing brigade ships in en masse. The drinks list, typed up like a long receipt, is a neat touch as is the suitably stylish outdoor terrace in summer. Look out for the frequent sushi nights when the glam set come in to pose their way through this new cult Ljubljana culinary craze.

**Pr Skelet** Ključavničarska 5; tel: 252 7799 [3 D5] **OT**

Delve below street level in the Old Town and you will soon be surrounded by an army of skulls and skeletons in this cellar bar. Once you get over the novelty of the horror theme it is not too disturbing and it is actually quite a fun bar, especially in summer when it is a respite from the buzzing action along the riverside above. In the colder months this is a cosy retreat for a glass of mulled wine. Those on a tight budget might even forgive the cheesy flyer that insists 'Yes, people are still dying to get in' after snapping up the all-day 2-for-1 cocktails.

**Raggamuffin** Krojaška 4 [3 D5] **OT**

Jamaica comes to town in the shape of Ljubljana's stab at a reggae bar. Black-and-white posters of Bob Marley may line the walls, but that distinctive smell is conspicuously absent and the interior is surprisingly bright and airy for a reggae bar. Curiously when we visited house music was on the stereo, but for a quieter retreat a block away from the bustling riverfront bars of the old town this is not a bad option.

**Romeo** Stari trg 6 [3 D6] **OT**
With the name and the pink neon lighting many visitors often mistake this former pizzeria for a gay bar, but do not be put off by the choice of décor at this Old Town option. Inside the high chairs are as funky as the music, while outside there is a sprinkling of tables and chairs that lead down towards the nearby river and an awning-covered wooden decking area, which is a perfect venue for people-watching. The food is good here too with all sorts of snacks and more substantial offerings.

**Salon** Trubarjeva 23; tel: 433 2006 [1 E4] **C**
One of the trendiest venues in the city underwent a touch-up recently and it is now looking great. One expat that we spoke to described it as 'lounge bar meets camp hairdressing salon', a remarkably apt summation. In summer a large terrace spills out onto the street outside. Once inside, the front area is a great place to relax on a faux leopard skin sofa and savour a hot chocolate – choose from dark, milk or white, or if you are really in the mood, the decadent 'chocolate fondue'. To the rear is a small bar that gives way to a larger lounge area where funky décor and projections liven things up. Beware the floor on the way to the toilets, which is frankly disturbing.

**Vinoteka Movia** Mestni trg 2; tel: 425 5448; www.movia.si [3 D5] **OT**
With Slovenia's better wines rarely available in supermarkets this is the place to come if you want to try a tipple or take home a bottle. This cosy wine bar next to the town hall is run by Movia, the wine producers from the southern wine region of Goriška Brdo, and some of their best vintages are on sale, including the excellent 1997 *Cabernet Sauvingon* at 6,000SIT a

bottle. The wines are stacked high up the wall behind the bar and many of them are available to taste before you buy. They also have some tapas-style nibbles with a hunk of the excellent Slovenian air-dried ham, *pršut*, tempting on the bar. If you fancy yourself as something of a wine connoisseur then this is the place to come as the friendly staff are always on hand to chat to you about Slovenia's myriad varieties, though popping in during the afternoon is the best idea so you get the chance to talk to them when it is not too busy.

**Zlata Ladjica** Jurčičev trg 1; tel: 241 0695 [3 D6] **C**
This popular bar by the Cobbler's Bridge suffers from schizophrenia as by day, especially at weekends, it buzzes with outdoor café life with everyone from students to families reclining by the river on the front and rear terraces. At nights things turn on their head as the action moves inside to a maritime-themed bar that is often one of the most raucous in the city, no wonder with Tennants Super, the lethal strength Scottish beer, on draught.

# 7 Entertainment and Nightlife

Slovenes take their cultural life so seriously that there is even a national holiday dedicated to culture – France Prešeren's birthday on February 8. During the Yugoslav days Ljubljana was always viewed as something of a cultural hub where experimental performance arts flourished and were given an impressively free rein by the authorities. This is after all the home of Slovenian national bard France Prešeren (see pages 18–19) and equally esteemed satirical writer Ivan Cankar, the man credited with establishing Slovene as a modern literary language, not to mention the first man to publish a book in the Slovene language, Primož Trubar.

Throughout the year the Slovenian capital bustles with the arts, ranging from small-scale street theatre and outdoor concerts, right through to grand opera performances, classical music recitals and the granddaddy of them all, the Ljubljana Summer Festival. Then there are the nightclubs – home to a smorgasbord of musical styles – with everything from grungy alternative sounds in Metelkova through to the current vogue for R&B which surfaces in Bachus.

Whatever your tastes there is something to suit everyone. All of Ljubljana's tourist offices hand out the free monthly *Where To* leaflet, which gives a good listings rundown, as well as a free A4 sheet detailing events on a weekly basis. For more alternative and small-scale events and happenings ask in trendy bars like Café Maček or Fraga. *Major Events in Ljubljana* is an annual publication that allows for a bit of advance planning if you can get hold of it.

## THEATRE

For a small city, Ljubljana has a decent supply of theatre venues which host a diverse range of performances. High-quality acting and vivid productions often transcend the language barrier and theatre groups to look out for include the Mladinsko Theatre, Betontanc, Koreodrama and the Ljubljana Dance Theater.

Most performances take place between 19.00 and 21.00, with any remaining tickets sold at the venue box office one hour before the show is due to start. Dress codes, like those in the city's restaurants, are smart casual, although some theatre- and opera-goers like to really dress up for the occasion. In most places jeans would not be out of place. Ticket prices vary and are tiered within many venues and range from 1,300SIT to 19,000SIT. Most performances come somewhere in the middle with seats costing 6,000–8,000SIT.

**Café Teater** Miklošičeva 2; tel: 252 7108; www.café-teater.si [1 D4] **C**
Theatre company specialising in musicals and comedy productions. Performances generally take place on weekends in the Križanke.

**Cankarjev Dom** Prešernova 10; tel: 241 7299; www.cd-cc.si. [3 B5] **C**
This 'Culture and Congress Centre' is one of the most popular and largest arts venues in Slovenia with a multitude of performances in two auditoriums, covering everything from theatre to classical music, dance and opera. Its information and booking office is open Mon–Sat 11.00–1300 and Mon–Fri 15.00–20.00 and then one hour before performances.

**Gledališče Glej** (Glej Theatre) Gregorčičeva 3l; tel: 421 9240 [3 B6] **C**
This is renowned as the most avant-garde venue with a daring programme geared towards more experimental material. Closed July and August.

**Križanke** Trg Francoske Revolucije 1; tel: 252 6544 [3 C6] **C**
This wonderful outdoor arena in a sculpture-laden old monastery is at the crux of the Ljubljana Summer Festival. The city's most romantic and atmospheric venue has a history that dates back to the 13th century, with church and monastery buildings from that era still standing today. Outside of the festival performances continue to take place in the outdoor arena, the Knights Hall and the anteroom. The venue is popular with visiting rock and pop groups, whose concerts clear the city centre, and is great for fans who can't get tickets as they can stand outside and literally feel the good vibrations.

**KUD Teater 55** Dunajska 113; tel: 041 555 555; www.teater55.com [off map] **OCC**
Small theatre company staging mainly comedy productions; performances generally take place at the Festivalna Dvorana Ljubljana and the Kulturni Dom Mengeš.

**Lutkovno Gledališče Ljubljana** (Ljubljana Puppet Theatre) Krekov trg 2; tel: 300 0970 or 080 2004 (ticket office); www.lgl.si [3 E5] **OT**
Not just for children, the theatre's ambitious programme ranges from A A Milne's *Winnie the Pooh* to Shakespeare productions. If you are in Ljubljana during the city's biennial International Puppet Theatre Festival make sure you catch one of the innovative puppet shows.

**Mestno Gledališče** (Municipal Theatre) Čopova 14; tel: 251 0852; www.mgl.si [1 C4] **C**
The diverse spectrum of performances on offer at the city's theatre includes satirical plays, comedies and modern theatre productions by budding Slovene and international playwrights.

**Mini Teater Ljubljana** Ljubljanski Grad; tel: 434 3620; www.mini-teater.si [1 E5:E6] **OT**
Ljubljana's castle provides an unusual and romantic setting for theatrical performances. The Mini Theatre also organises the city's Medieval Day with Renaissance music, puppet shows, battle re-enactments and plays.

**Šentjakobsko Gledališče** (St Jacob Theatre) Krekov trg 2; tel: 231 2860; www.sentjakobsko-gledalisce.si [3 E5] **OT**
The performance list of this alternative theatre group includes Monty Python's *Life of Brian*, Jules Verne's *20,000 Leagues Under the Sea*, as well as the work of Slovene playwright Ivan Cankar.

**Slovensko Mladinsko Gledališče** (Slovenian Youth Theatre) Vilharjeva 11; tel: 231 0610; www.mladinsko-gl.si [1 E1] **OCC**
Established in 1955, the Slovenian Youth Theatre prides itself on its eclectic range of mainstream and experimental productions. Past performances have included works by Chekhov, Dostoyevsky, Lewis Carroll and T S Elliot.

**Slovensko Narodno Gledališče Drama** (Slovenian National Drama Theatre) Erjačeva 1; tel: 252 1511; www.sngdrama-lj.si [3 C5] **C**
Slovenia's national theatre company is enviably housed in this lavish art-nouveau building.

**Teater Komedija** (Comedy Theatre) Šmartinska 152; tel: 585 1432; www.btc.si [off map] **OCC**

By night the BTC City Convention Hall plays host to comic productions.

## CINEMA

Many of the city's cinemas show films in English with Slovene subtitles and relatively few are dubbed. The mainstream cinemas show a similar range of Hollywood films that you would find anywhere else in Europe, though the local appetite for all things alternative spills over at the Slovenska Kinoteka and the Kinodovr with their more varied celluloid fare. In November each year the city also plays host to the Ljubljana International Film Festival (LIFFe); www.liffe.spletnastran.com and the Ljubljana Gay and Lesbian Film Festival.

**Kinodvor** Kolodvorska 13; tel: 434 2544; www.kinodvor.si [1 E3] **C**

Shows contemporary art-house films that have received wide critical acclaim such as Sue Brooks's *Japanese Story*. During the summer the cinema also screens Slovene-language films with English subtitles.

**Kolosej** Šmartinska 152; tel: 520 5500; www.btc.si [off map] **OCC**

Part of the suburban BTC City complex, Slovenia's first multiplex cinema has 12 screens, a bar, restaurant and confectionery store.

**Slovenska Kinoteka** Miklošičeva 38; tel: 434 2500; www.kinoteka.si [1 D3] **C**

This cinema, which specialises in art-house productions, closed towards the end of 2004, but the TIC assured us that it would reopen after a refurbishment in time to celebrate 100 years of Slovenian film in 2005 (see *Sightseeing*).

## MUSIC

Music abounds in Ljubljana, particularly during the Ljubljana Summer Festival (see *Culture and festivals*). In summer Centralni Stadion (Central Stadium) and Križanke

### LJUBLJANA SUMMER FESTIVAL

The Ljubljana Summer Festival has been going strong since 1952 and now embraces most of the city's performance spaces in a cultural extravaganza that rumbles through July and August. The key venue is the Križanke, but Ljubljana Castle, Cankarjev Dom and the Slovene Philharmonic Hall all come into play with myriad events. In 2004 guests included the London Symphony Orchestra, NHK Tokyo Symphony Orchestra and the Moscow Soloists Chamber Orchestra. The surrounding countries are also embraced with 2004 bringing in the Croatian National Theatre, as well as the National Theatre of Belgrade. The latter's choice of *Jekyll and Hyde* seemed strangely apposite to many locals who have lived through the Yugoslav wars of the 1990s and Serbia's recent struggle to emerge from being a hardline Slobodan Miloševic-run state into a modern democracy.

are unique and atmospheric venues for performances. In winter the action moves indoors to intimate venues like Križanke's Knights Hall and the ornate surrounds of the Slovene Philharmonic Hall. The latter celebrated its 300th anniversary in 2003 and is the third oldest of its kind in Europe, with the orchestra and choir based there proud of their worldwide reputation.

Other key classical music groups include the RTV Slovenia Symphony Orchestra and the Slovenian Chamber Orchestra. The former has received wide international acclaim, featuring regularly on BBC Radio 3 in the UK and other radio stations around the world. Slovenia's national opera and theatre companies are also based in Ljubljana, with regular performances taking place at the Slovenian National Opera and Ballet Theatre.

Numerous small gigs, geared towards the city's large student population, also take place. Diverse venues include those in Metelkova, an artistic compound that sums up the musical spirit of Ljubljana, as what is now a creative musical hub used to be an oppressive military barracks. Big one-off events include the Ljubljana Jazz Festival and the Druga Godba festival (see *Culture and festivals*); the latter showcases alternative music, with grunge rock bands and creative world music combos taking the stage.

Tickets for a string of events can be purchased from the box office of individual venues, and increasingly over the internet.

## Classical and opera venues

**Cankarjev Dom** (see *Theatre*)

**Križanke** (see *Theatre*)

**Slovenska Filharmonija** (The Slovenian Philharmonic Hall) Kongresni trg 10; tel: 241 0800; www.filharmonija.si [3 C5] **C**
One of the most atmospheric venues in the country is home to the Slovenian Philharmonic Orchestra and the Slovenian Philharmonic Choir. Dramatic frescos and organs add to the charm of the Great Hall, whilst the intimate ambience of the Small Hall has an allure of its own (see *Sightseeing*).

**Slovensko Narodno Gledališče Opera in Balet** (Slovenian National Opera and Ballet Theatre) Cankarjeva 11; tel: 241 1740; www.operainbalet-lj.si [1 B4] **C**
Traditional and contemporary opera and ballet productions grace the stage of this old-world theatre. Past recitals have included Puccini's *Tosca* and Verdi's *Trubadur*, as well as works by Johann Strauss and Sergei Prokofiev (see *Sightseeing*).

## Rock, pop and jazz venues

**Centralni Stadion** (Central Stadium) Dunajska [off map] **OCC**
This tatty suburban football stadium is a decent venue for larger concerts – Lenny Kravitz played here in 2004.

**Jazz Club Gajo** Beethovnova 8; tel: 425 3206; www.jazzclubgajo.com [1 C4] **C**
This centrally located jazz club in the embassy district has regular live performances and weekly informal jam sessions, with the latter generally held on Monday evenings. The club

post their monthly schedule online. There are rumours that the club will be forced to change venues in the near future.

**Križanke Summer Theatre** (see *Theatre*) **KT**
Scene of numerous summer concerts including the Pixies and Kraftwerk in 2004.

**KUD France Prešeren** Karunova 14; tel: 283 2288; www.kud-fp.si [3 C8] **KT**
This popular youth venue prides itself on promoting alternative culture, with music performances, theatre and art that veers away from the mainstream dominating the calendar. Literary and educational events are also staged here, as are events for children.

**Metelkova Mesto** (see *Clubbing culture*) [2 G3] **OCC**
Everything from bangra and African tribal groups, through to nu-metal and rap. Multiple venues in the squat itself, combined with the concerts at the Gala Hala in Tivoli Park it arranges, means that there is always something happening.

**Orto Bar** Grabloviceva 1; tel: 232 1674; www.orto-bar.com [2 J2] **OCC**
One of the city's leading live-music venues hosts bands playing everything from blues and jazz to punk and trash. The bar's signature red velvet lounge may be a characterful venue, but it can also get very smoky.

**Sax Pub** Eipprova 7; tel: 283 9009 [3 C8] **KT**
This Trnovo mainstay serves up a solid menu of live jazz every Thursday evening. The interior is cosy and feels more like a music lover's bedroom than a pub with CD racks lining the walls and various memorabilia dotted around. Arrive early if you want a seat

when there is music. At other times this is a relaxed place for a drink amidst a slightly older and very relaxed crowd.

**ŠKUC Information Centre** Stari trg 21; tel: 121 3142 [3 D6] **OT**
Old Town ticket outlet for concerts in Ljubljana.

## CLUBBING CULTURE

**Bachus Center** Kongresni trg 3; tel: 241 8244; www.Bachus-center.com [3 C5] **C**
While Bachus is often less trendy and hip than it thinks it is, this sprawling modern venue can be a lot of fun. The owners have made the most of an excellent location and have put a lot of work into a well-designed complex that offers a café, a sprinkling of bars, restaurant and even a pool hall, as well as a basement dancefloor. On a good night Bachus buzzes, but on busy weekends it can seem to be full of underagers and big egos clad in ill-fitting R&B clobber, and the queues to get in can be a nightmare.

**Discoteka Fun Factory** Industrijska cona Rudnik, Jurčkova 224; tel: 428 9690; www.discoteka-funfactory.com [off map] **OCC**
*B/9 direction Livada*
South of the city centre in Rudnik is Ljubljana's biggest club. Here you will find all the things you expect in large clubs, like chill-out rooms, multiple bars and separate dancefloors.

**Global** Tomšičeva 1; tel: 426 9017; www.global.si [1 C4] **C**
Take the elevator from street level at the Nama department store and less than a minute later you will be in this modern nightlife oasis with sweeping views of the city centre and

the castle. The terrace is open during the day as a café/restaurant, but the real action is inside at night on the single dancefloor. To the left is a small bar and to the right is a VIP area – reserved for members and those lucky enough to wangle their way onto the guest list – with tables that overlook the city. The music policy is a bit hit and miss – on our last visit the funky youths of Ljubljana were not posing to the latest sounds, but instead were getting on down to Duran Duran, disco and early 1990s cheesy house. Check ahead if you don't want to find yourself at a weird and wacky theme night.

**Klub Central** Dalmatinova 15; tel: 200 8740 [1 D4:E4] **C**
This once-popular club that once pumped out cheesy disco to a youthful crowd of locals and tourists has re-emerged, after a refit as a fairly pricey gentleman's club.

**Klub K4** Kersnikova 4; tel: 431 7010; www.klubk4.org [1 C3] **C**
K4 was pumping out cutting-edge sounds when Global and Bachus were only pipe dreams and it is still going strong well over a decade since it first opened its doors. The dingy and grungy rooms echo the nefarious hideouts of East Berlin and the music is similarly alternative with indie rock and metal ruling. K4 is nothing if not flexible, though, and on our last visit they had British progressive trance DJs in with the local student population lapping them up.

**Latino Klub Cuba** Celovška 54; tel: 434 3158 [off map] **OCC**
*B1 direction Vižmarje, B5 direction Podutik, B8 direction Brod, B15 direction Medvode and B16 direction Gameljne*

Latino beats, salsa music and free-flowing cocktails are all winning ingredients in this popular club at Casa del Papa outside the city centre.

**Metelkova Mesto** Metelkova; tel: 432 3378; www.metelkova.org [2 G3] **OCC**
This independent and unique cultural centre can easily keep visitors occupied on a night out. A predominantly young and alternative Slovene crowd are drawn to the clubs and bars that inject life into this former military barracks and squat. Venues include Klub Gromka, with live music and international DJ's and Klub Channel Zero, where heavy metal, punk, hardcore and trance reign supreme. The squat also has a gay nightlife scene (see *Gay Listings*)

**Papillon** Nazorjeva 6; tel: 426 2126 [1 D4] **C**
Techno dominates Papillon's music scene at the weekend, whilst retro nights are the order of the day during the week. This idiosyncratic venue is one of Ljubljana's most bizarre. Upstairs in the club itself the namesake film is played in a continuous loop, whilst décor in both the nightclub and the downstairs restaurant also keep with the film's theme and are styled as a French colonial prison.

**Sub Sub Club** Celovška 25; tel: 515 3575 [1 B2] **TK**
Part of the Hala Tivoli, this centrally located club is popular with the dance music crowd. Opening times vary so it is wise to look out for flyers and posters.

## GAY LISTINGS

**Fraga** (see *Bars and Wine Bars*)
Gay friendly café at the heart of the Old Town.

**Kavarna Planet Pločnik** (see *Cafés*)
Gay friendly café on Prešernov trg.

**Klub Monkel** (see *Clubbing Culture*)
This lesbian nightclub, located in the Metelkova squat, shares its premises with Tiffany's.

**Klub Tiffany** (see *Clubbing Culture*)
Metelkova's gay and lesbian café-bar cum club is a welcoming oasis just outside the city centre.

**K4 Roza** (see *Clubbing Culture*)
Sunday is K4's gay night, transforming the grungy student venue into the 'Roza Klub'.

# Shopping

8

Ljubljana is a good city for shopping despite some frustrating opening hours. Its compact size means that dedicated shoppers can cover the entire city centre on foot. Slovenska, which bisects the city centre, with its big-name shops and the Nama department store is one popular shopping boulevard. However, a far more pleasant experience is on offer in the Old Town squares of Stari trg, Mestni trg and Gornji trg, where medieval and baroque buildings house eclectic boutique shops selling everything from jewellery, perfume, shoes and clothes to traditional crafts and designer gear made in studios behind the stores. The right and left banks of the Ljubljanica River are also increasingly brimming with boutique stores and small art galleries. Gosposvetska cesta, near the Lev hotel, also has some boutiques.

## ANTIQUES

**Antika Ferjan** Mestni trg 21; tel: 426 1815 [3 D6] **OT**

**Antikvariat Novak** Kongresni trg 1; tel: 426 7141 [3 C5] **C**

**Antikvariat Tizian** Ključavničarska 3; tel: 425 0048 [3 D5] **OT**

**Carniola Antiqua** Trubarjeva 9; tel: 231 6397 [1 D4] **C**

**Galerija Ars** Juričičev trg 2; tel: 241 4760 [3 D6] **C**

### *OPENING HOURS*

The only downside of shopping in Ljubljana is the infuriating weekend opening hours. Thanks to a referendum held on September 21 2003 shops in the capital close at 12.00 or 13.00 on Saturday afternoons and do not open again until 08.00 or 09.00 on Monday morning, playing havoc with retail-addict city-breakers. Shop hours are usually 09.00–19.00 Monday–Friday and 09.00–13.00 Saturday, although some shops may open and close an hour earlier.

Those in need of a retail fix will be pleased to discover that some of the city's department stores do open on Saturday afternoons, and that stores in the BTC City mall, 3km out of town, welcome customers until 20.00 on Saturday evenings and until 13.00 on Sundays, although local pressure groups are campaigning to curtail these opening hours.



## ARTS, CRAFTS, GIFTS AND SOUVENIRS (*see Galleries*)

**Artglass Atelje** Dvorni trg 2; tel: 426 3104 [3 D6] **C**

Stylish studio selling beautiful glassware products made by Slovene designer Tomaž Miletič.

**Ažbe Galerija** Mestni trg 18/II; tel: 425 1337; fax: 425 8811; www.galerija-azbe.si [3 D5] **OT**

Open Mon–Fri 10.00–13.00 and 16.00–19.00, Sat 10.00–13.00.

A wonderful collection of paintings, antiques, glass, silverware and bric-a-brac, displayed in traditional glass-fronted cabinets.

**Dom** Mestni trg 24; tel: 241 8300 [3 D5] **OT**

Large souvenir shop housed in a municipal building with wicker, wood, pottery and woollen crafts on sale, alongside alcohol and a wide range of Ljubljana-labelled souvenirs.

**Galerija** Dvorni trg 2; tel: 426 4097 [3 D6] **C**

Browse the paintings on sale in this gallery, which is also a popular bar.

**Galerija Idrijske Čipke** Gornji trg; tel: 425 0051 [3 D6] **OT**

Small gallery selling a wide selection of handmade lace from Idrija. There are also occasional lace-making demonstrations.

**Prodnajalna Na Trgu** Ciril Metodov trg 5; tel: 234 7630 [3 E5] **OT**

A smaller branch of Dom selling similar products.

**Rustika Gallery** Ljubljanska Grad [3 E5] **OT**

The arts and crafts on sale in Ljubljana Castle's gallery, are well crafted and typically Slovenian. Highlights include Idrija lace, ceramics, glassware and woodwork. These high-quality souvenirs have prices to match.

**Skrina Galerija** Breg 8; tel: 425 5161; fax: 425 8503; www.skrina.si [3 D6] **C**

Charming riverside gallery selling paintings and artistic souvenirs aimed primarily at tourists. Idrija lace, Prekmurje pottery, Rogaška glass and beehive panels are all amongst the traditional Slovenian crafts. It is cheaper to pay by cash than credit card.

**TIC** Stritarjeva ulica; tel: 306 1215 [3 D5] **C**
The tourist office sells a range of quality tourist souvenirs, from Ljubljana dragon sculptures and scenic pictures, to candle holders and clay door hangings, all carrying the TIC's official Ljubljana Souvenir stamp.

**Trgovina Medex** Miklošičeva 30; tel: 431 6116 [1 D4] **C**
A great place to stock up on Slovenian honey, beeswax candles, honey pastries and even honey dough ornaments.

**Trgovina Tendence, Rogaška Crystal** Šmartinska 152; tel: 521 1740 [off map] **OCC**
*B2 direction Nove Jarše or B7 or B17 direction Letališka*
Lead crystal glasses and other glassware made at the Rogaška Dekor workshop in the northeast of Slovenia. This franchised outlet is part of the BTC City complex.

**Urar Bazelj** Cankarjevo nabrežje 3 [3 D5] **OT**
Step back 50 years in this delightful old-world clock shop.

## BOOKS

**Geonavtik** Kongresni trg 1; tel: 252 7027 [3 C5] **C**
Friendly bookstore-cum-café.

**Knjigarna Novak** Wolfova 8; tel: 422 3410 [3 D5] **C**
This small, friendly and centrally located bookshop sells a selection of English and other foreign-language books.

**Mladinska Knjiga** Slovenska 29; tel: 241 0651 [3 C5] **C**
The biggest of the Mladinska Knjiga stores, sells a selection of English-language books, at a price.

**Mladinska Knjiga** Nazorjeva 1; tel: 241 4700 [1 D4] **C**
With English-language titles.

## CLOTHING

**Hugo Boss** Slovenska 41; tel: 252 7789 [1 C3] **C**
Good-sized shop selling men's designer clothing.

**Katarina Silk** Gornji trg 5; tel: 425 0010 [3 D6] **OT**
Stylish silk scarves and other items are handcrafted on the premises.

**Mass** Čopova 14; tel: 200 8680 [1 D4] **C**
An abundance of affordable shoes are on sale in this large shop which spans two floors.

**Max Mara** Miklošičeva 6; tel: 426 5880 [1 D4] **C**
Elegant designer clothing store for women located opposite the Grand Union Hotel.

**NAF NAF** Nazorjeva 2; tel: 241 5690 [1 D4] **C**
Designer fashion retailer with prices slightly lower than many other cities in western Europe.

**Pletilni Studio Draž** Gornji trg 9; tel: 426 6041 [3 D6] **OT**
Stunning viscose and cotton dresses are made in the studio behind the shop.

**Sisley** Čopova 7 [1 C4] **C**
Decent-sized branch of this Italian designer-clothes retailer for men and women.

**Transport** Čopova 3 [1 D4] **C**
The New York City street map that adorns the façade makes this fashionable shoe shop easy to find.

**Zara** Slovenska 33; tel: 421 4500 [1 C4] **C**
Large outlet for women's designer clothing.

## DEPARTMENT STORES/SHOPPING CENTRES

**BTC City** Šmartinska 152; tel: 585 1100; www.btc-city.com [off map] **OCC**
Open Mon–Sat 09.00–20.00, Sun 09.00–13.00.
*B17 direction Letališka to BTC uprava stop*
This enormous shopping mall, located northeast of the city centre in Moste, boasts over 400 shops including Top Shop, Top Man, Miss Selfridge, Levi's and Benetton. It also has myriad sports facilities including tennis, badminton, go-karting and a swimming pool, restaurants, multiplex cinema and a comedy theatre.

**BTC Emporium** Letališka 3; tel: 585 4800; www.emporium.si [off map] **OCC**
*B17 direction Letališka to BTC Emporium stop*
This shopping centre is a haven for those who love buying clothes. High-street names like Dorothy Perkins, Burton, Levi's, Mexx, Timberland, Dockers and Jockey sell their wares alongside Hugo Boss and Hugo Boss Woman, Lacoste and Fred Perry.

**Maximarket** Trg Republike 1; tel: 476 6800; www.maxi.si [3 B5] **C**
Department store selling everything from perfume, wine and CDs to golf equipment, especially busy on Saturday afternoons (it is open until 17.00) when the majority of the city's other stores have closed for the weekend.

**Metalka** Dalmatinova 2; tel: 431 1155; www.metalka.net [1 D4] **C**
Large department store that sells everything from large household appliances and bathroom suites to confectionery and tobacco. Perhaps more useful to the overseas visitors are the sports equipment and clothing departments. You might also pick up gifts here, with a choice of cosmetics, jewellery, glass, crystal and porcelain.

**Müller** Čopova 40; tel: 200 2400 [1 C4] **C**
This dated department store is a good place to stock up on cheap toiletries. It also sells toys and CDs.

**Nama** Tomišičeva 1; tel: 425 8300 [1 C4] **C**
The large United Colours of Benetton outlet, on the ground floor, is one of the department store's biggest attractions.

## FOOD AND WINE

**Mercator** Kongresni trg 9; tel: 241 4770 [3 C5] **C**
A central branch of this omnipresent supermarket chain that is open on Sundays.

**Mercator** Stritarjeva 9; tel: 241 4089 [3 D5] **OT**
Another centrally located Mercator. Closed on Sundays.

**Plečnik colonnades** Adamič-Lundrovo nabrežje [3 D5:E5] **OT**
The small shops selling bread, honey, cheese, wine, ham and fish are a great place to stock up on Slovenian produce. They are also good places to buy honey as a gift to take home.

**Vino Boutique** Slovenska 38; tel: 425 6280 [1 D3] **C**
Small wine shop with knowledgeable staff.

**Vinoteka Bradeško** Gospodarsko (Fairgrounds), Razstavišče-Jurček Pavilion, Dunajska 18; tel: 431 5015 [1 D1:E1] **OCC**
Under the expert guidance of owner Simon Bradeško staff here really know their wine. The huge variety of Slovenian wines on sale and the opportunity to dine in the fantastic cellar restaurant make the short journey to this Ljubljana institution well worthwhile.

**Vinoteka Movia** Mestni trg 1; tel: 425 8119 [3 D5] **OT**
Trendy wine bar and shop owned by the well-known Movia wine producer.

## JEWELLERY

**Dragulji Malalan** Mestni trg 19; tel: 421 7740 [3 D5] **OT**
This upmarket jeweller has been trading in Ljubljana for over 50 years and is the place to buy a new watch. Designer brands on sale include Tag Heuer, Omega, Zenith, Lorenz, Emporio Armani and Pierre Balmain.

**Kamen** Stari trg 32; tel: 426 9975 [3 D6] **OT**
Modern chunky pieces made with stones, beads, metal and silver. Kamen also has a small selection of unusual gifts including clocks.

**Kodre Zlatarstvo** Cankarjevo nabrežje 27; tel: 422 5110 [3 D5] **OT**
Chunky rings and bracelets, dangling pendants and oversized looped earrings, are just some of the individual pieces by Slovene designers guaranteed to get you noticed.

**Mladi Malalan** Pod Trančo 5; tel: 251 9537 [3 D6] **OT**
With the same owners and similar products to Dragulji Malalan.

**Ruby and Sapphire Lanka** Gornji trg 10; tel: 425 1462 [3 D6] **OT**
Elegant boutique selling jewellery from Sri Lanka including contemporary pieces with precious or semi-precious stones set in silver, or more traditional gold rings and pendants.

## MARKETS

**Flea Market** Cankarjevo nabrežje [3 D5] **OT**
This Sunday morning market lines the Ljubljanica between the Triple Bridge and the Cobbler's Bridge.

**Ljubljana Monmarte** Cankarjevo nabrežje [3 D5] **OT**
On Saturdays from June–September the banks of the Ljubljanica are once again transformed into a market. This time arts and crafts are on sale between 10.00 and 15.00. A highlight for younger visitors are the creative workshops that are held as part of the market.

**Tržnica (Central Market)** Vodnikov trg and Pogačarjev trg [3 E5] **OT**
Open daily except Sunday this is a great place to pick up cheap produce, flowers, clothes and even a small selection of souvenirs including wooden crafts and honey.

## OUTDOOR/SPORTS

**ProMontana** Poljanski nasip; tel: 280 0590; www.promontana.si [4 F5] **C**
This travel agency specialising in outdoor activities has a retail outlet in the capital, which sells and rents out equipment and clothing for various outdoor pursuits. They can also provide you with information about the company's programme of activities, including mountaineering, hiking, mountain biking and paragliding in the Julian Alps.

# Walking Tour

9

As there are a lot of attractions to cover and the Ljubljanica River neatly divides the city in two, the walking tour is split likewise, with the route on the left bank a bit longer but less hilly than that on the right. It is possible to cover both walks in one long day, but this does not allow for any time at all in the museums and galleries. Ideally take at least a full day to explore each bank, enjoying a decent lunch in the middle and a liberal sprinkling of coffee stops to allow yourself the luxury of soaking up the relaxed ambience of the city. Both tours start at the tourist information centre on Stritarjeva, where you can pick up a map, and end at the central Prešernov trg.

## RIGHT BANK TOUR

From the TIC follow the river northeast back along Plečnik's dramatic colonnades to the **Tržnica** (Central Market – see *Sightseeing*) on Podgarčarjev trg. From Monday to Saturday this area buzzes with life during the day and its myriad stalls, shops and food outlets are a great place to have a quick bite to eat. Take time to wander amongst the stalls in a world as far away from supermarket hegemony as you are likely to find in Europe today. This is a great place for taking photos too. The market spills on to neighbouring Vodnikov trg, which also houses the voluminous **Cerkev Sv Nikolaja** (Cathedral of St Nicholas – see *Sightseeing*), with its frescos by Giulio Quaglio and its impressive dome, painted by Matevž Langus.

Back towards the river from the cathedral continue along the colonnades and at the next river crossing you will come to the **Zmajski Most** (Dragon Bridge – see *Sightseeing*), with four big vicious-looking green dragons and a litter of smaller ones, the famous symbols of the city, standing guard. If you need to check your emails pop into the Slovenian Tourist Information Centre at Krekov trg around the corner just before the bridge. On the opposite side of the square is the **Lutkovno Gledališče Ljubljana** (Ljubljana Puppet Theatre – see *Theatre*); while across busy Reslieva is Plečnik's very own **Peglezen** ('Flatiron' Building), perhaps not one of his finest works.

So far you have just been catching glimpses of **Ljubljanski Grad** (Ljubljana Castle – see *Sightseeing*) as it hangs high above the Old Town, but now it is time to venture up to this sturdy fortress. There are plans for a new funicular that will spirit visitors up from Krekov trg, but for now the most appealing route up to the castle is on Študentovska, which snakes up in a flourish of cobbles on a surprisingly steep ascent from Vodnikov trg. Trees soon crowd all around, but between the branches, and in winter when the leaves are gone, you can snatch sweeping views of the city and start to appreciate just how surrounded by mountains and hills the Slovenian capital is.

Once inside the castle reward yourself with a refreshing drink at Bar Grad (see *Cafés*) and take in the various architectural styles on display. For a deeper insight into the city's history take the virtual reality 3D tour before regrouping for the descent back into the Old Town's cobweb of streets. For a more 'real' experience head up the castle's tower, where sweeping views of the city and the Julian Alps stretch out into the distance.

## GREEN LJUBLJANA

So intent are the local tourist authorities on keeping the capital clean and green that they dreamed up the 'Making Ljubljana More Beautiful' project in 2003. Local students were encouraged to take a hands-on approach and take part in an orgy of litter lifting and graffiti scrubbing as the city was given a decent nip and tuck. The project returned in 2004 and now seems set to be an annual push. In April 2004 it was also joined by an effort to clean up the Ljubljanica with citizens, expats and tourists alike all encouraged to participate in a fun day sprucing up the city's river.

Follow the same path you came up on until you are just below the castle ramparts, where there is a fork to the left. This leads down in a circuitous swirl towards Gornji trg, which is fast becoming one of the smartest streets in the city with upmarket restaurants and boutique shops. This baroque boulevard is one of the parts of Ljubljana that helps conjure up all of those Prague comparisons and you really could be strolling through the heart of the Czech capital. At the foot of Gornji trg, where you will come across a copy of the Hercules Fountain (the original is in the town hall) avoid the temptation to skip past the **Cerkev Sv Jakob** (Church of St James – see *Sightseeing*) and make the effort to divert left and discover this 17th-century church, whose altar was modelled by Francesco Robba.

Plečnik hated the church and many locals reckon he had the voluminous trees, which today drown out the façade, planted especially to hide it.

It is just a short stroll back to Stari trg, which together with Mestni trg forms the core of the Old Town and are its busiest squares. Most of the buildings on the narrow cobbled thoroughfare are baroque, but astute visitors may notice that a few of them have not been knocked through to make larger buildings and still retain their compact original medieval structure.

Follow the welter of small shops, bars and cafés that spring up along Stari trg and the transition to Mestni trg is seamless. Soon you will come to the impressive **Rotovž** (town hall –see *Sightseeing*) on the right. Delve inside into the Gothic courtyard to check out the relief of Ljubljana and also the paintings that depict various stages of the city's history. Just across from the town hall is Robba's famous 'Fountain of the Three Carniolan Rivers' (see *Sightseeing*), which was recently unveiled after a revamp. It depicts the city's three lifeblood rivers and you are bound now for one of them, the Ljubljanica, where Plečnik's remarkable **Tromostovje** (Triple Bridge – see *Sightseeing*) can be seen ready to spirit you back across to Prešernov trg where you can congratulate yourself on your efforts in one of the cafés or bars.

## LEFT BANK TOUR

From the TIC cross the Triple Bridge and cut south along the river – you are now on the left bank of the Ljubljanica in the more modern part of the city centre.

Continue past the uninteresting modern narrow footbridge and the next one you come to is another Plečnik creation, the **Čevljarski Most** (Cobbler's Bridge – see *Sightseeing*). To the right is the tiny old Jewish quarter, basically the narrow streets of Židovska ulica and Židovska steža, in an area now alive with cafés and galleries.

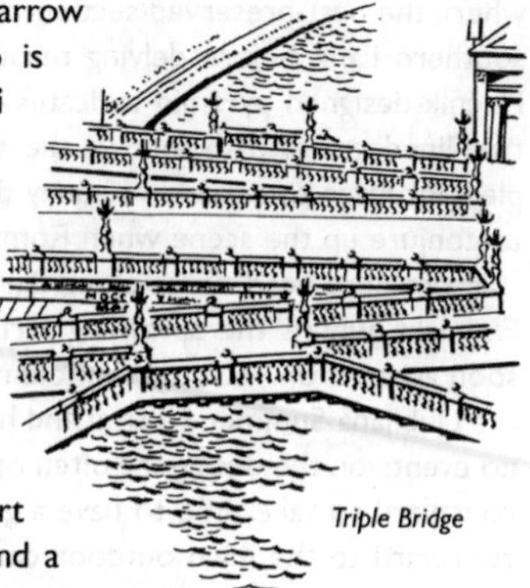

Sticking to the river the banks soon become Breg, where Ljubljana's main harbour once lay when the Ljubljanica was the city's lifeblood. Breg kicks off with a new art gallery/café, Breg 2 (see *Bars and wine bars*), and a string of smart furniture stores, before opening up to Novi trg to the right. This is one of the city's least-visited main squares, but is worth at least a quick look with a smattering of 18th- and 19th-century buildings. At the top you will catch sight of the striking National and University Library; more on that later.

*Triple Bridge*

Continue on Breg until you come to the large road bridge. Do not cross it – instead keep walking into the suburb of Krakovo on Kravokvski nasip. Turn right up Krakovska and you will feel like you have entered a time warp with old ladies tending to their vegetable gardens. Another time warp awaits when you cut left at the top of Krakovksa; wander south down Emonska and turn right onto Mirje where the best-preserved section of Ljubljana's Roman walls lie. Walk first up their southern flank before delving through the most westerly of Plečnik's gates. The Plečnik-designed pyramid indicates the height of the wall during Roman times. A tree-lined gravel path follows the section of wall back to where you started, a pleasant place to relax on a sunny day – sit for a minute and you may just be able to conjure up the scene when Romans patrolled these walls.

From here head north along Barjanska, turn right along Zoisova and left on to Emonska where the sprawling **Križanke** complex (see *Sightseeing* and *Theatre*) soon appears on your right, an old monastery that is now a cultural oasis, home to the Ljubljana Summer Festival and host to many big concerts. Even when there are no events on the doors are often open and in summer there is a simple café in the courtyard so take time to have a good look around and delve further behind the courtyard to the main outdoor concert arena. From Križanke turn right and you will come straight to the impressively renovated **Mestni Muzej** (City Museum – see *Sightseeing*), which is housed in the grand Auersperg Palace.

Back on Rimska head back up to towards Trg Francoske Revolucije, where you will find the only memorial to Napoleon outside of France, a large column that is a legacy of the days when Ljubljana was the capital of the general's short-lived Illyrian Provinces. If it is a sunny day you may want to stop for a coffee at the relaxed Le Petit Café (see *Cafés*), but if you are more interested in Plečnik than relaxing turn right at the roundabout back towards the city centre on Vegova, where his influence is strongly felt.

The first building on Vegova on the right is generally regarded as Plečnik's greatest achievement: the **Narodna in Univerzitetna Knjižnica** (National and University Library – see *Sightseeing*). Even the beautifully designed bronze doors clearly show his touch. There are tours that are meant only for prospective members if you are feeling cheeky, but anyone is allowed into the main staircase, vestibule and the stylish café in the basement, so you can get a feel for the place without having to break the rules. Towards the end of Vegova look out for the **Glasbena Matica** (School of Music), with what is clearly another Plečnik façade, this time with various Slovenian composers depicted on it.

The Plečnik theme continues as you spill into the expanse of Kongresni trg (see *Sightseeing*), where EU membership was celebrated in 2004. The square boasts buildings from many major time periods during the city's history and both the Roman and medieval walls of Ljubljana ran through the square. A flurry of grand structures crowd around the green park in the centre, with the dominant building being the headquarters of the **Univerza v Ljubljani** (University of Ljubljana – see *Sightseeing*) this former palace has a bust of Plečnik sitting by the entrance (the middle bust as you look over the wall from Vegova).

To the east towards the river is the **Slovenska Filharmonija** (Slovene Philharmonic Hall – see *Sightseeing* and *Theatre*), while at the other flank of the square is the unusual 18th-century pillared façade of the **Uršlinska Cerkev Sv Trojice** (Ursuline Church of the Holy Trinity – see *Sightseeing*), where you should head after you have had a good look at the other buildings and checked out any events on the square itself. The park is laid out in a star shape and the sleek modern café at the northeastern fringe, Zvezda (see *Cafés*), translates appositely as 'star' in Slovene; a good place to stop if you need a break.

Next to the Ursuline Church of the Holy Trinity to the west is a passageway that spills out into Trg Republike, the largest square in the city and either a grand testament to socialist-era architecture or a hideous concrete monstrosity depending on your tastes. Here you will find the **Cankarjev Dom** cultural centre (see *Theatre*), in all its functional glory. Much of the square is blighted by parked cars, but the sculpted façade of the **Državni Zabor** (National Assembly) catches the eye to the north. This solid building was the work of Vinko Glanz in the 1950s, while the recently refurbished heroic sculptures were added by Karel Putrih and Zdenko Kalin. This was where President Milan Kučan made his emotive speech on June 26 1991, as the country lay on the brink of both independence and war, declaring 'This evening dreams are allowed – tomorrow is a new day.'

Heading west out of the square through the park on Subičeva, next up is the **Narodni Muzej Slovenije** (National Museum – see *Sightseeing*), a wonderfully old-fashioned museum, the oldest in Slovenia, that can swallow up a few hours with its permanent and temporary collections, not to mention its grand staircases and palatial feel. Behind the gallery are two interesting buildings in the diplomatic quarter: the Russian (Tomšičeva ulica 9) and American (Prešernova 31) embassies. Ljubljana has to be fairly unique in the world in that these two embassies are right next to each other, which must be lot of fun for their inhabitants trying to listen over the garden fence and sneak around while the others are out.

Just a block further north is the **Moderna Galerija** (Museum of Modern Art – see *Sightseeing*), an impressive hub in a nondescript building that caters for the local penchant for all things experimental and eclectic. If you enjoy your modern art set aside time for a separate visit here. Across the road from this temple of the avant garde a more classical oasis awaits with the **Narodna Galerija** (National Gallery – see *Sightseeing*) just to the north, an impressively vast place, built in the 19th century, that just manages to steer on the right side of stuffy, though again if you want to really explore it come back later. If you are just walking past you can see the marked difference between the older stone and newer glass sections of the gallery.

If it is a hot day or if you just fancy a respite from trudging around the streets pop over busy Tivolska to Tivoli Park using the pedestrian underpass that is visible from outside the two galleries. This green lung is awash with pathways, trees and flowers and is perfect for idle strolling with a rumble of grand buildings, fountains and a sports complex to explore as well. The **Muzej Novejše Zgodovine** (Museum of Modern History – see *Sightseeing*) also lies within Tivoli. If you are really feeling energetic you can wind your way around the myriad trails that run through the park from here, taking in the views of the city as you gain altitude.

Heading back towards the city centre take the underpass again and note the **Srbska Pravoslavna Cerkev** (Serbian Orthodox Church – see *Sightseeing*) –

dedicated to saints Cyril and Methodius – which is a pretty unusual religious edifice for Slovenia, never mind Ljubljana. This distinctly Serbian Orthodox church is awash with ornate domes on its exterior, while its interior is brightened up with murals. Continue back along Cankarjeva and you will soon come to the **Slovensko Narodno Gledališče Opera in Balet** (Slovenian National Opera and Ballet Theatre – see *Sightseeing* and *Classical and opera venues*) on the right, which looks like it was purpose-built, but was actually opened originally as a theatre.

Continue east until you hit bustling Slovenska, turn left and within a block you will see the **Nebotičnik**, the city's first skyscraper and, when it was opened in 1933, the tallest building in the Kingdom of the Serbs, Croats and Slovenes. Sadly the observation level and café were closed at the time of going to press as a wrangle of ownership and development rights continues with little sign of a solution.

From this striking tower cross Slovenska and continue north before turning right down Dalmatinova. This brings you to Miklošičev Park (see *Sightseeing*), with its collage of impressive art nouveau buildings. After you have had a good look turn right out of the southeast corner of the square and you are on Miklošičeva, where the fine art nouveau buildings continue. Keep your eyes rooted firmly upwards as you head down towards the river and admire the grand façades with the highlights the cream extravaganza of the Grand Hotel Union Executive at number 1, easily the most attractive hotel in the city, and the Nekdanja Zadružna Gospodarska Banka (Commercial Cooperative Bank) at number 8 with its zany geometric design and bright colours. From here the last thing to see is the proudly pink façade of the **Frančiškanska Cerkev Marijinega Oznanjenja** (Franciscan Church of the Annunciation – see *Sightseeing*) as you spill into Prešernov trg and the end of the walk.

10

# Sightseeing

## THE UNMISSABLES

**Prešernov trg** (Prešeren Square) [1 D4] **C**

Prešernov trg is at the physical, historical and spiritual heart of the city. This is where *Ljubljančani* come to meet their friends, watch the world go by in pavement cafés and stroll by the river. The square boasts three river crossings, the landmark **Frančiškanska Cerkev Marijinega Oznanjenja** (Franciscan Church of the Annunciation – see *Churches and cathedrals*) and a statue of poet France Prešeren. Ivan Zajec's and Maks Fabiani's dramatic monument to the man trumpeted as Slovenia's greatest bard dates from 1905. Despite his bravado and his swirling muse the tortured writer is forced to gaze across his namesake square at a bust of Julija Primic, the love of his life. Julija may be peering back at Prešeren, but in real life she never returned his love, and many see her presence as a cruel and constant reminder of this most tragic of tragic romantic poets and his unrequited love. Julija aside, the steps of

*Prešeren statue*

this giant statue make a great place to relax with an ice-cream or to meet some new friends.

As well as being the most popular meeting spot in the city, Prešernov trg boasts some of Ljubljana's finest examples of art nouveau architecture. The large white building standing proudly behind Prešeren is the oldest *lekarna* (pharmacy) in Ljubljana (refurbished in 2004), while the city's first department store – the Centromerkur – sits to its left. On the opposite side of the square is the Hauptman House, now also owned by Centromerkur. Look out also for the bronze model of the city, which has been at the bottom of Čopova since June 26 1991 when Slovenian independence was declared.

Ljubljana's most vibrant square also sees the coming together of two of Slovenia's most famous sons, France Prešeren and Jože Plečnik, with the designs of the latter giving the square its modern-day appearance. One of Plečnik's most famous works, **Tromostovje** (the Triple Bridge), was completed in 1931 with the addition of two straddling walkways to the main 19th-century span. Plečnik wanted to mimic the bridges that traverse Venice's canals, incorporating ornate Renaissance balustrades and a string of street lamps into his flamboyant design.

In summer there are regular concerts in the square. On busy weekdays, when traffic rattles past at an alarming rate, Prešernov trg loses some of its charm, but on sunny weekends when all of Ljubljana seems to be cruising over the Triple Bridge with an ice-cream in hand, or late at night when spotlighting gives it an ethereal glow, its appeal re-emerges.

**Ljubljanski Grad** (Ljubljana Castle) Tel: 232 9994; www.festival-lj.si/virtualnimuzej [3 D5:D6] **OT**
***Castle*** Open daily 10.00–21.00 Oct–Apr; daily 09.00–22.00 May–Sep. Admission free. Tours: 10.00 and 16.00 Jun–mid Sep or by arrangement.
***Virtual Museum and Viewing Tower*** Open daily 10.00–21.00 Oct–Apr; daily 09.00–21.00 May–Sep. Admission 700SIT, concessions 400SIT, family ticket 900SIT.
Ljubljana Castle hangs omnipresent above the city, vaulting into view when you turn many a street corner. If you are feeling lazy there is a tourist train up here from Prešernov trg (see *Local tour operators*), but a better option is to walk up the steep slopes and see the view start to unravel below. Recent excavations have shown signs of settlement as far back as the 12th century BC, but the castle was first fortified by the Celts and the Illyrians. Later the Romans also capitalised on the highly strategic location, with sweeping vistas right out over the whole city and up towards the Julian and Kamniške Savinje Alps.

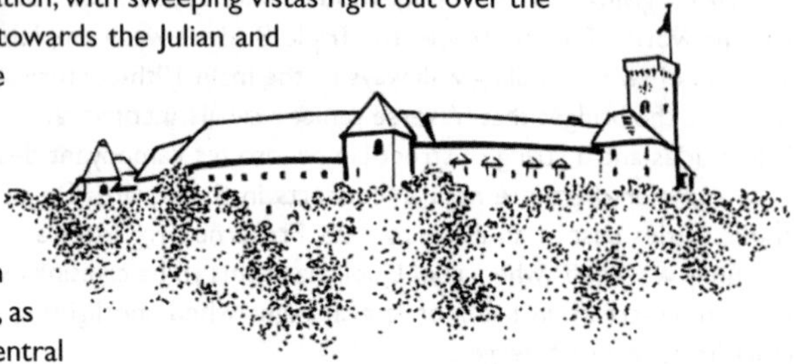

In many ways the medieval fortress is more impressive from the outside than in, as once inside the central

## *THINGS TO LOVE AND HATE ABOUT LJUBLJANA*

(Culled from the thoughts of a random sample of expats living in the city during an evening in the Cutty Sark pub – see *Bars and wine bars*.)

| **Love** | **Hate** |
|---|---|
| Strolling around the city centre | The city centre being used as a giant car park |
| Clean and green city | The rain |
| Cycling around | Crazed cyclists trying to mow you down |
| The food | The food |
| The boutique shops | Shops closing at weekends |
| Central Market | Supermarkets sprouting up everywhere |
| Greasy *bureks* | Greasy *burek* guilt |
| Tivoli and Krajinski parks | Concrete socialist architecture |
| Friendly locals | Shop staff chatting to friends while you wait |
| NUK library | NUK reading room being closed to visitors |

courtyard the shamble of buildings date from different periods, with a truly hideous 1960s functional section that has already aged badly. The 15th-century remnants are more appealing and there are a flurry of things to keep you occupied including a café, a well-stocked gift shop with souvenirs from all over the country, a tower with a great view and a multimedia exhibit. The latter runs visitors through a 3D history of the city, tracing its development vividly from its Roman days as Emona, right through its grand baroque era to the 1980s. The 20-minute show is well timed to avoid boredom setting in and even if you normally shy away from multimedia shows this is worth it. The castle is also home to a string of cultural and religious events, including Sunday masses in summer, Ljubljana Summer Festival events and New Year's fireworks. From June to September the castle's history is brought to life by knowledgeable guides who lead visitors through various halls, the chapel and the dungeon.

**Mestni trg, Stari trg and Gornji trg** (Town Square, Old Square and Upper Square) [3 D5:D6] **OT**

These connecting squares, which hug the base of Castle Hill, ripple through the heart of the Old Town in a flurry of appealing baroque and medieval buildings. Many of the city's most popular cafés, bars and restaurants are located in or around these long squares, which buzz with life. Even the advent of supermarket chains and out-of-town malls has failed to kill off the impressive array of boutique shops and small businesses that keep the area alive.

**Ljubljanica**

The Ljubljanica may not be as impressive and grand as some of Europe's great rivers, but what is often little more than a sleepy stream can churn into quite a lively rush of water after heavy rain or snow melts. Boat tours of the river recently started and now leave just across from Prešernov trg on the Old Town side with guided commentary. Strolling along the riverbanks is equally rewarding with a constantly changing view of the city. From Prešernov trg try walking south by the banks and after you enter the Trnovo district you will come to the riverbanks that were designed by Jože Plečnik (see *Krakovo and Trnovo*). This is a great place to relax on a balmy summer's day or to work off the cobwebs on a crisp winter's afternoon. From here you can cross to the Prule district and meander back up the river to the Old Town on the tree-shrouded lanes.

As well as being central to the social lives of the *Ljubljančani*, the attractive banks of the Ljubljanica also harbour some of the city's most impressive sights. The concrete riverbanks themselves are the work of Ljubljana's most influential architect, with Plečnik altering the river's course to prevent flooding. The steep concrete banks that predominate in the heart of the city are brightened up by trees, bright flowers, wrought-iron dragons, well-planned street lighting and even temporary art exhibitions. Plečnik also constructed the **Čevljarski Most** (Cobbler's Bridge) – so named because it was the location where cobblers once sold their wares – with its balustrades and tall lampposts. Taking time to study the medieval and baroque dwellings that line the riverbanks reveals ornate coving, wrought-iron balconies and arched doorways, as well as colourful though often-faded façades. Heading east along the river beyond the market brings you to the **Zmajski Most** (Dragon Bridge – see pages 181–2).

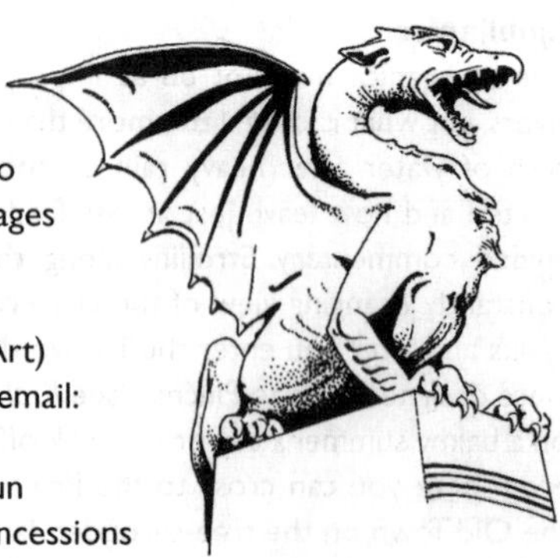

**Moderna Galerija** (Museum of Modern Art)
Tomšičeva 14; tel: 241 6800; fax: 251 4120; email: info@mg-lj.si; www.mg-lj.si [1 B4] **C**
Open Tue–Sun 12.00–20.00 Jul–Aug; Tue–Sun 10.00–18.00 Sep–Jun. Admission 800SIT, concessions 600SIT; free Sat.

This is one of Ljubljana's true joys and lovers of avant garde art should make a beeline for this gallery and allow plenty of time. Even if your tastes are more traditional it is well worth looking around for some interesting domestic artists and a variety of temporary exhibits and, as it is only a stone's throw from the National Gallery, you can combine both in a contrasting visit.

The building itself looks quite forbidding from the outside, but is spacious and flexible inside with an exhibition space on the ground floor as well as additional galleries in the basement. Edvard Ravnikas was the Slovene architect behind the building, completed in 1939 as war erupted across Europe, with definite Plečnik influences clearly discernible. The main focus of the permanent collection is on Slovenian art from the 20th century, but the temporary exhibits draw on both domestic and international talents. Other activities include art workshops, discussion groups and the publications the gallery produces on Slovenian art. The gallery also owns the Mala Galerija (Small Gallery) and exhibition space at Metelkova 22.

## MUSEUMS

**Narodni Muzej Slovenije** (National Museum of Slovenia) Muzejska 1; tel: 241 4404; fax: 241 4422; email: info@narmuz-lj.si; www.narmuz-lj.si [1 B4] **C**
Open Tue, Wed and Fri–Sun 10.00–18.00, Thu 10.00–20.00. Admission 700SIT, concessions 500SIT, children 400SIT; free 1st Sun of month. Combination ticket covering entrance to the National Museum of Slovenia and the Slovenian Museum of Natural History 1,000SIT, concessions 700SIT.

Housed in a stunning neo-Renaissance palace, the museum's façade is impressive. The National Museum also has a striking vestibule with ornate frescos and an attractive stone and marble staircase with banisters adorned by white statues. Considering the size of the building the museum exhibits are surprisingly small. The permanent collection on the ground floor is displayed in corridors around a central courtyard, and consists mainly of stone relics and reliefs from Slovenia's Roman period. Descriptions of the artefacts are in both Slovene and English. As you travel through the exhibits you will also encounter an attractive Roman mosaic and a handful of Egyptian artefacts including a mummy, reputedly the only one in Slovenia. Signs on this level are confusing and actually lead to offices or closed rooms and are often best ignored.

Having quickly exhausted the ground-floor exhibits head up the staircase and take the right branch when it splits, a spot marked by a bust of Prešeren. The left staircase will take you to the Natural History Museum, which shares the same building (see following listing). When we last visited there were two galleries open, one of which had an engaging display of prehistoric glass and amber from different regions of Slovenia. Large and informative boards in both Slovene in English provided information about the objects, their origins and the regions they were found. Attractive jewellery and beads, including very small beads shaped as ram heads, were displayed inside glass-fronted cabinets, with some English-language translations. Although temporary the exhibition showed what could be made of this space.

**Prirodsoslovni Muzej Slovenije** (Slovenian Museum of Natural History)
Prešernova 20 (entrance Muzejska 1); tel: 241 0940; fax: 241 0953; email: uprava@pms-lj.si; www.2pms-lj.si [1 B4] **C**
Open Fri–Wed 10.00–18.00 and Thu 10.00–20.00. Admission 500SIT, concessions 400SIT, ISIC card holders free; free 1st Sun of month. Combination ticket covering entrance to the National Museum of Slovenia and the Slovenian Museum of Natural History 1,000SIT, concessions 700SIT.

A taxidermist's dream, this old-school Natural History Museum brims with stuffed mammals and amphibians. It also has a large collection of skeletons and a visually striking photographic exhibition of Slovenia's fauna and flora. It may be old fashioned, but children love it. Highlights for younger visitors include more than 300 different varieties of bird – including a griffon vulture, golden eagle and white-tailed eagle – huge bears, stags and a wild boar. There is also a sizeable display of stuffed fish, including a shark and an enormous salmon. Not all of the exhibits have been conserved by taxidermy, with poisonous snakes pickling in preservative jars. A gruesome display of bones, including a human skeleton, the skeleton of a dog and the skulls of a gorilla and an antelope, and the skeletal reconstruction of an enormous woolly mammoth, also fascinate children visiting the museum.

One highlight for older visitors are the stunning pictures of Triglav National Park, which form part of the display of Slovenia's natural environment. In other galleries myriad varieties of rocks and minerals hint at the country's diverse geology.

**Mestni Muzej** (City Museum of Ljubljana) Gosposka 15; tel: 252 2930; email: info@mm-lj.si; www.mm-lj.si [3 C6] **C**
Open Tue–Sun 10.00–18.00. Admission free.
Until it closed for renovation in 2000 the City Museum was one of Ljubljana's most popular museums. It reopened to much fanfare in 2004, but its permanent collections were not put back on display immediately, with plans mooted to roll them out by the summer of 2005. Until they all return visitors can admire the sheer

beauty of the building and its brilliant refurbishment, walk amongst Roman ruins, including a section of old Roman road, and watch projections of the planned permanent exhibition. In addition there are regular temporary shows, some of them delving into the history of the city as the museum did before the revamp. The Auersperg Palace, in which the museum is housed, is multi-functional with children's workshops, adult classes, as well as a congress hall and a relaxed café. When the permanent collection is installed it will follow the evolution of the city, the Auersperg family and the *Ljubljančani*.

**Slovenska Kinoteka** Miklošičeva 28; tel: 434 2520; fax: 434 2521; email: kinoteka@kionteka.si; www.kinoteka.si [1 D3] **C**
Part cinema and part museum, the Kinoteka, when fully functioning, exhibits artefacts and documents from cinematic history and has a regular schedule of retro and art-house cinema from Slovenia and around the globe. It is also a venue for annual film festivals such as the Ljubljana Film Festival and the annual Lesbian and Gay Film Festival (see *Culture and festivals*). Closed for renovation in September 2004 local sources say the Kinoteka is set to reopen to celebrate the 100th anniversary of Slovenian film-making in 2005.

**Arhitekturni Muzej Plečnik** (Architectural Museum Plečnik Collection)
Karunova 4; tel: 280 1600; email: pz@aml.si; www.arhmuz.com [3 C8] **KT**
Open Tue and Thu 10.00–14.00. Admission 600SIT, concessions 300SIT.

Plečnik devotees must make the pilgrimage to the architect's beloved Trnovo house, which is located near the Church of St John the Baptist in Trnovo. The building, which Plečnik made his home for 40 years, now comes under the auspices of the Architectural Museum. Most of the house is open to visitors, including his bedroom, drawing room and studio. The Winter Garden is currently used for Plečnik study groups.

**Slovenski Šolski Muzej** (Slovenian School Museum) Plečnikov trg 1; tel: 251 3024; email: solski.muzej@guest.arnes.si; www.ssolski-muzej.si [3 C4] **C**
Open Mon–Fri 09.00–13.00. Admission free.
Reopened in September 2004 after a renovation, this museum is primarily of interest to Slovene speakers and education enthusiasts. This specialised collection essentially looks at the history of teaching in Slovenia, teaching methods and aids, the evolution of schools and classroom furniture. Photographs of Slovenian schools through the centuries are also part of the collection, as are over 55,000 educational titles, which are kept in the museum's library.

**Pivovarski Muzej** (Brewery Museum) Pivovarniska 2; tel: 471 7340; email: pivovarski.muzej@pivo-union.si; www.pivo-union.si [1 C1:C2] **OCC**
Open by appointment, first Tue of month 08.00–13.00. Admission free.
If your interest in Union, Ljubljana's home-grown beer, is insatiable and you can round up a group then you will be able to go on an organised tour at the Union

Brewery, where there is a small museum dedicated to the hallowed brew. If you want to visit the brewery call ahead. The museum website was not working at time of research.

**Tobačna Muzej** (Tobacco Museum) Tobačna 5; tel: 477 7344; fax: 477 7155; email: tobacna@tobacna.si; www.tobacna.si [1 A5] **OCC**
Open 10.00–18.00 every 1st Wed and 3rd Thu of the month or by appointment. Admission free.
Very visual exhibits trace the history of tobacco production from the time that the tobacco plant was first discovered in America through to its exportation to Europe and Slovenia. Even in the absence of English translations visitors can learn a surprising amount about the development of the Ljubljana Tobacco Company, where the museum is housed. Ornate snuffboxes, cigarette holders and pipes are also on display.

**Slovenski Etnografski Muzej** (Slovenian Ethnographic Museum) Metelkova 2; tel: 432 5403; email: etnomuz@etno-muzej.si; www.etno-muzej.si [2 G3] **OCC**
Open daily 10.00–18.00, extended hours to 20.00 on Thu. Admision free.
Since 2002 activity at the museum has been restricted to occasional exhibitions and events, due to the construction of a new museum building. Scheduled to reopen fully in 2005, exhibitions in the new building will give an insight into traditional Slovenian life through folk art, artefacts from rural life, folk craft and displays based

around trade, textiles, home furnishings and architecture. The museum will also have a collection of artefacts from around the world, with a focus on North America and Africa.

**Muzej Novejše Zgodovine** (Museum of Modern History) Celovška 23; tel: 300 9610; fax: 433 8244; www.muzej-nz.si [1 A1:A2] **TK**
Open Tue–Sun 10.00–18.00. Admission 500SIT, concessions 300SIT, free first Sun of month.
A range of audio-visual effects, photographs and fascinating artefacts take you on a journey through Slovenia's modern history, from the beginning of World War I in 1914 to the country's declaration of independence in 1991. The collection resides in the attractively restored 18th-century Cekin mansion on the outskirts of Tivoli Park. The remains of the Yugoslav army helicopter shot down over the city vividly evoke the 1991 war.

**Železniški Muzej** (Railway Museum) Parmova 35 and Kurilniška 3; tel: 291 2641; www.burger.si/MuzejiInGalerije/ZelezniskiMuzej/Uvod.html [1 C1] **OCC**
Open Mon–Thu 10.00–13.00. Admission free.
Rail buffs will not want to miss the rail museum in a country whose railways have a fascinating history. As well as old photos of the network that was largely put together by the Austro–Hungarians when they governed Slovenia, there are also hulking great train engines and accompanying wagons. For such a small

country and city the array of over 60 locomotives is pretty impressive. Note the museum is spread across two sites which are within walking distance of each other.

**Arhitekturni Muzej** (Architectural Museum) Fužine Castle, Pot na Fužine 2; tel: 540 9798; email: aml@aml.si; www.arhmuz.com [off map] **OCC**
Open Tue–Sun 11.00–19.00. Admission 300SIT, concessions 150SIT.
The main collection of the Architectural Museum is dramatically housed in a Renaissance mansion. Given the significant focus on Jože Plečnik it is tempting to think of this as a Plečnik museum, but in fact the works of many other modern Slovenian architects are covered including Ivo Spinčič, France Tomažič, Ivo Medved, and Vinko Glanz. The various departments of the museum encompass industrial design, visual and electronic media and photography, with explorations also into the history of Fužine Castle itself as well as regular temporary exhibitions. Town planners or architects wanting to spend an afternoon on a busman's holiday may want to delve into the comprehensive library, though much of the material is in Slovene. The permanent Plečnik collection is an edited version of the large exhibition staged at the Pompidou Centre in Paris in 1986, which covers all his main periods from his days in Vienna and Prague, through to his seminal work in Slovenia. Some of the most interesting exhibits are plans by the prolific architect for further additions to his beloved Ljubljana.

**Experimentov Hiša** (Experiment House) Trubarjeva 39; tel: 300 6888; email: info@h-e.si; www.h-e.si [2 F4] **C**

Open Sat and Sun 11.00–19.00.

This unusual venue gives children and adults alike the chance to interact with 30 scientific exhibits, including dancing liquid and helium balloons. Largely booked up by school groups during the week, visitors are invited to drop in at weekends.

## GALLERIES

**Narodna Galerija** (National Gallery), Prešerova 24; tel: 241 5434; fax: 241 5403; email: info@ng-slo.si; www.ng-slo.si [1 B4] **C**

Open Tue–Sun 10.00–18.00. Admission 800SIT, concessions 600SIT.

Designed by Škrabout, from the Czech Republic, and constructed a year after the 1895 earthquake as the National House, Slovenia's biggest art gallery boasts an impressive collection of sculptures and paintings that date from the Middle Ages through to the late 19th century. It also has an interesting photographic collection that gives a pictorial history of Slovenia. The gallery has recently been expanded, and the addition of a northern wing has added a collection of works by European masters to those of well-known Slovene artists like Jakopič, Kobilca and Metzinger.

**Mestna Galerija** (City Gallery) Mestni trg 5; tel: 241 1770; email: mestna.galerija-lj@siol.net; www.mestna-galerija.si [3 D5] **OT**

Open Tue–Fri 10.00–18.00, Sat 10.00–13.00 Sep–Jun, Tue–Sat 10.00–14.00 and 17.00–20.00, Sun 10.00–13.00 Jul and Aug. Admission free.
Not content with having one location the City Gallery manages to spread its eclectic wings across four sites, two of them in the heart of the city and two in the suburb of Bežigrad. In the original three-level building (Mestna 1) on Mestni trg is a gallery with around a dozen temporary exhibitions a year. Nearby on Cankarjevo nabrežje is the gallery's permanent collection (Mestna 2), which houses nearly 200 works of art by both Slovene and international artists. There are two further galleries in Bežigrad, each with their own temporary exhibitions. The first on Dunajska was brought under the wing of the City Gallery in 1996 and like its patron holds around a dozen exhibitions a year. Many exhibits tend to focus on installations, 'concrete poetry' and other multimedia projects. Although founded in 1976 the second Bežigrad branch also came on board in 1996 with a similar emphasis in its exhibitions.

***Mestna 2*** Cankarjevo nabrežje 11/I; tel: 241 1790; www.mestna-galerija.si [3 D5] **OT**

***Bežigrad Gallery 1*** Dunajska 31; tel: 436 6957; www.mestna-galerija.si [off map] **OCC**

***Bežigrad Gallery 2*** Vodnova 3; tel: 436 4057; www.mestna-galerija.si [off map] **OCC**

**Commerce Galerija** Einspielerjeva 6; tel: 309 4175; fax: 436 9476; email: galerija@commerce-lj.si; www.commerce-lj.si [off map] **OCC**
Open Mon–Fri 09.00–17.00. Admission free.

This Slovenian company has its hand in the food and beverage, textiles, plastics and real-estate industries. One of its more unusual ventures is the art gallery situated at the company's head office. Regular exhibitions showcase the works of talented Slovenian artists, with paintings and sculpture displayed in a light and modern space.

**Tivoli Gallery** Grad Tivoli, Pod turnom 3; tel: 241 3800; www.mglc-lj.si [off map] **TK**
Open Wed–Sun 11.00–18.00. Admission free.
Also known as the International Centre of Graphic Art, this gallery, housed in the Tivoli Mansion, is primarily concerned with printmaking; the centre also stages frequent graphic art exhibitions and organises the Ljubljana Graphic Arts Biennial.

**Cankarjev Dom Gallery** Prešernova 10; tel: 241 7100; www.cd-cc.si [3 B5] **C**
Open Tue–Sat 10.00–19.00 and Sun 10.00–14.00. Admission free.
Staging diverse exhibitions throughout the year by Slovenian and international artists, recent works have included photography, painting on canvas and coloured-glass creations.

**Mala Galerija** (Small Gallery) Slovenska 35; tel: 251 4106; www.mg-lj.si [1 C4] **C**
Open Tue–Sat 10.00–1800 and Sun 10.00–13.00. Admission free.
This bijou gallery showcases emerging domestic talent and is well worth popping into.

**ŠKUC Galerija** Stari trg 21; tel/fax: 421 3140; email: galerija.skuc@guest.arnes.si; www.galerija.skuc-drustvo.si [3 D6] **OT**
Open Tue–Sun 10.00–20.00. Admission free.
Part of the ŠKUC Cultural Centre, this Old Town gallery has been showcasing avant-garde Slovenian art since 1978.

**DESSA Architectural Gallery** Židovska steza 4; tel: 251 6010; fax: 421 7975; email: ljdessa1@guest.arnes.si [3 C6] **C**
Open Mon–Fri 10.00–15.00. Admission free.
The gallery of The Association of Freelance Architects (DESSA) arranges around ten architectural exhibitions each year in a suitably stylish space designed by Boris Podrecca.

**ZDSLU Gallery** Komenskega 8; tel: 433 0380; fax: 434 9462; email: info@zveza-dslu.si; zveza-dslu.si [1 E4] **C**
Open Mon–Fri 10.00–18.00. Admission free.
Varied exhibitions by members of the Union of Slovene Fine Artists include black-and-white photography, sculpture and eclectic paintings and drawings.

**Fotografija Galerija** Petkovškov nabrežje 47; tel: 430 2519 [4 F5] **C**
Open Mon–Fri 10.00–19.00, Sat 10.00–13.00. Admission free.
Constantly changing photographic exhibitions.

**Luwigana** Gornji trg 19; tel: 252 7369 [3 D6] **OT**
Open Mon–Fri 11.00–19.00, Sat 10.00–13.00. Admission free.
Old Town establishment selling works by Slovene and international artists.

**Galerija Hest** Židovska 8; tel: 422 0000; www.galerijahest-sp.si [3 C6] **C**
Open Mon–Fri 10.00–14.00 and 15.30–20.00, Sat 10.00–13.00. Admission free.
A light and spacious gallery tucked behind the video shop on Juričičev trg, exhibiting contemporary art.

**Galerija Hest 35** Novi trg 6; tel: 426 2168; www.galerijahest-sp.si [3 C6] **C**
Open Mon–Fri 10.00–14.00 and 15.30–20.00, Sat 10.00–13.00. Admission free.
Modern art gallery on the same street and with the same owners as the Galerija Hest.

## SITES AND MONUMENTS

**Nebotičnik** (Skyscraper) Slovenska 37 [1 C4] **C**
Ljubljana's original skyscraper was the tallest building in Yugoslavia when it was constructed in 1933. A café once tempted at the top of the building offering stunning views of the city's skyline. For now visitors have to content themselves with a street-level exploration as a debate centred around denationalisation has led to its closure and there is little to suggest it will reopen soon. If you head a little further south down Slovenska to the Nama department store, at Tomšičeva

1, and take the lift to the Global café and nightclub on the fifth floor, you can get a similar view.

**Miklošičeva and Miklošičev Park** [1 D3:D4] **C**

In the streets immediately north of Prešernov trg visitors will discover a profusion of historically and culturally significant buildings that were constructed after the earthquake that devastated the city in 1895. Josip Vancaš's great art nouveau structure, the **Grand Hotel Union Executive** at Miklošičeva 1, was opened in 1905, having taken just 18 months to complete. In addition to its striking art-nouveau exterior the hotel boasts etched-glass window panes and an elegant interior that retains many period features. Opposite the hotel at Miklošičeva 4 is the **Slovenska Zadružna Kmetijska Banka** (People's Loan Bank), with its intricate decorations, symbols, blue tiles and attractive figures, two of which sit on the roof. The Max Mara clothing store (Miklošičeva 6) features intricate detail below the roof and understated tiles that frame its arched windows.

More immediately striking is the former **Nekdanja Zadružna Gospodarska Banka** (Commercial Co-operative Bank) created by Ivan Vurnik – which is located opposite the hotel at number 8. Vurnik's wife, Helen, gave him a helping hand and is credited with painting it from head to toe in a vibrant pink and with its doors and windows framed by elaborate rusty red, yellow, blue and white geometric patterns. Ljubljana's most colourful building is especially impressive on a bright sunny day. One question, though, continues to perplex those who come to admire it: just how do you fit the whole building into your camera viewfinder?

Other impressive buildings on this side are the **Bambergova Hiša** (Bamberg House) at Miklošičeva 16 – look out for the ceramic reliefs of some of Slovenia's most renowned painters – the **Krisperjeva Hiša** (Krisper House) at Miklošičeva 20 and **Regali Hiša** (Regali House), at Miklošičeva 18. The first two secessionist structures are the masterpieces of Maks Fabiani who was commissioned to rebuild the area around Miklošičev Park, or Slovenska trg (Slovene Square) as it was formerly known, in the early 20th century. Fran Berneker is the architect behind Regali's House. The former workers' chamber – notable for the seven marble figures, sculpted by Lojze Dolinar, that adorn the roof – is at Miklošičeva 28, the present-day location of the Slovenska Kinoteka (see *Cinema* and *Museums*).

On the western side of Miklošičev Park you can see two more examples of art-nouveau architecture. Sadly the first, the green façade of the **Čudnova Hiša** (Chuden House), is looking slightly worse for wear. Presiding over the park from Tavčarjeva 9 is the second, Ljubljana's court building. Notable features of this expansive neo-classical structure include the four columns that stand tall over the main entrance, its balconied windows and the intricate geometric brickwork. Look out also for the clock on the right gatepost that still tells the correct time.

Immediately opposite the courthouse you will see the statue of Franc Miklošič himself. The story of how the Slovene professor of Slavic studies came to be there is perhaps more interesting that the somewhat incongruous statue. The statue's pedestal was originally home to Austro–Hungarian Emperor Franz Josef, who was later replaced by figureheads from the Socialist Federal Republic of Yugoslavia. Tired of constantly replacing the heads of state that resided here, the city authorities decided that the effigy should be neutral.

**Tržnica** (Central Market) [3 E5] **OT**
The Tržnica is a defiant stand against global hegemony. Some locals rue the fact the resellers and larger operators are starting to muscle in, but amongst the colourful stalls you will still find old ladies from Trnovo and Krakovo selling fresh fruit and vegetables that they have cut that morning from their allotments. No visit to Ljubljana is complete without coming here. Try to eat here at least once, snacking on a *burek* or some fresh fruit, or popping into the more permanent shops amongst the colonnades on the river side of the market that dish up their own delights. Organic is a term that does not really apply here as almost everything is and it comes as a surprise to many visitors to discover that tomatoes can actually be more than just red balls of water, as they seem to be in supermarkets in many European countries.

The best time to visit the market, which fills Vodnikov trg and the smaller Pogarčarjev trg, is on Saturday, when it seems like the whole city has turned out and brightly coloured and strongly scented flowers abound. On Pogarčarjev trg you will also find the **Stolna Cerkev Sv Nikolaja** (St Nicholas's Cathedral – see *Churches and Cathedrals*) and the **Škofijski Dvorec** (Bishop's Palace). Constructed in 1512 this is one of Ljubljana's oldest buildings. In the five centuries since its construction it has played host to many eminent Europeans, with Napoleon Bonaparte and the Russian Tsar Alexander I rumoured to be amongst them.

The square is also home to the **Semenišče** (Seminary) that dates from the beginning of the 18th century. Two hulking stone giants, carved by sculptor Angelo Pozzo, guard the Seminary's south portal. The real beauty of this theological college, though, lies in its library – an impressive combination of breathtaking Giulio Quaglio frescos and baroque furnishings. Viewing of the library is by appointment only, as the academy is still used today, and these can be arranged at the Ljubljana TIC.

Even if you don't intend to do any shopping a visit to the market is a must as it is home to Jože Plečnik's wonderful colonnades, the riverside arcade of columns built in 1939–40 which follows the gentle curve of the Ljubljanica and conceals an impressive number of small shops selling fresh cheese, meat and baked goods, as well as an underground fish market and the great-value Ribca restaurant (see *Restaurants*).

**Zmajski Most** (Dragon Bridge) [1 E4] **C/OT**

The first concrete and iron bridge to cross the Ljubljanica is located at the northern end of Plečnik's colonnades and was erected to commemorate the 40th anniversary of Austro–Hungarian emperor Franz Josef's accession to the throne (1848–88). Designed in secessionist style by Juriji Zaninović, a Croatian architect who studied at the Wagner School in Vienna, and constructed in 1900–01, the bridge's chief attractions are the four large green dragons that sit in each corner and the smaller dragons that guard the bridge's lights. Local legend claims that the dragons will wag their tails when a virgin crosses the bridge; others have somewhat cruelly nicknamed this impressive structure the 'Mother-in-Law' due to its fiery nature.

**Mestni trg** (Town Square) [3 D5:D6] **OT**
Perhaps the smartest of Ljubljana's three Old Town squares, Mestni trg owes much of its contemporary appearance to the baroque period of the late 17th and early 18th century. Here amongst the beautiful façades and courtyards of ancient palaces and middle-class houses you will find the seat of the city council, a smattering of expensive shops and some of the city's most refined bars and restaurants. As you walk down the street remember to look up to really appreciate the intricacies of the square's ornate façades – particularly noteworthy is the **Souvanova Hiša** (Souvan House) at number 24.

**Rotovž** (Town Hall) Mestni trg 1; tel: 306 3000 [3 D5] **OT**
Atrium open Mon–Fri 09.00–19.00. Admission free.
There have been buildings on this site as far back as the 15th century, but most of today's baroque structure was conjured up by Gregor Maček in 1718. Although the town hall still functions as a seat of power, tourists can flit amongst some of its most interesting parts. Key features to look out for are the external balcony,

pentagonal clocktower, interior courtyard, Gothic entrance hall, the patterned arches of the baroque arcade, the auditorium and the Hercules and Narcissus fountain, which was the work of Robba's workshop.

**Robba's Fountain** [3 D5] **OT**
Another of Robba's attractive fountains – the Fountain of the Three Carniolan Rivers – stands resplendent outside the town hall. Having recently been brought back to its best with a comprehensive renovation, this vaulting masterpiece depicts the three great rivers of Carniola: the Krka, Ljubljanica and the sweeping Sava. Each of the rivers has been personified by a mighty Triton pouring out water from large jugs. A number of visitors have suggested that Robba got his idea for the 1751 masterpiece from Italian artist Gian Lorenzo Bernini, who created the Fountain of the Four Rivers, which can be found in Rome's Piazza Navona. Plans have been mooted to relocate the fountain to Prešernova ulica, outside the National Gallery.

**Riblji trg** (Fish Market Square) [3 D5] **OT**
This compact square, linking Mestni trg to the Ljubljanica, is entered through a small arch and boasts some of the oldest dwellings in the city. According to the plaque on house number 2, now the Abecedarium café (see *Cafés*), the building was constructed in 1528. For many Slovenes the house is important not because of its age, but as the former home of Primož Trubar (see *History*) who is said to have resided there in the 16th century.

**Stari trg** (Old Square) [3 D6] **OT**

The main attractions on Stari trg are its bountiful cafés, restaurants, bars and shops, but if you can drag yourself away there are a number of buildings worth exploring. Look out for the beautiful wrought iron-balcony, the bust of Slovene poet Lili Novy and the particularly impressive baroque frontage on the Schwieger House at number 11a.

**Levstikov trg** (Levstik Square) [3 D6] **OT**

The focal point of this attractive square, which received a Plečnik makeover in the early 1930s, is the **Sv Jakob Cerkev** (Church of St James – see *Churches and cathedrals*). Outside the church is the Shrine to Mary, which was placed here in 1681 as a thank you to God, when the Turks bypassed Ljubljana. Across traffic- clogged Karlovška is the **Gruberjeva Palača** (Gruber Palace), which is widely regarded as one of Ljubljana's most impressive examples of late baroque architecture. Constructed by Gabriel Gruber between 1773 and 1781 the building boasts a dome-capped oval stucco staircase, and its own first-floor chapel complete with frescos by Kremser Schmidt depicting scenes from the life of the Virgin Mary.

**Gornji trg** (Upper Square) [3 D6:E6:E7] **OT**

A raft of baroque and medieval dwellings climb gently eastward away from Stari trg and Levstikov trg on what is arguably Ljubljana's most attractive street, Gornji trg. Only a few of the houses retain their original medieval style; these can be identified by three windows running across the width of the building, while those with more windows have been combined and have taken on a later baroque style. Walking up the street immerse yourself in window-shopping with myriad handmade gifts, antiques and ornate jewellery amongst the offerings. Just beyond the midway point the highlight is the **Cerkev Sv Florijana** (Church of St Florian – see *Churches and cathedrals*).

**Kongresni trg** (Congress Square) [3 C5] **C**
This grand square was constructed in 1821 to commemorate the formation of the Holy Alliance, although it was later restyled by Plečnik. Just one block back from the Ljubljanica, it is a place where the locals gather for free concerts and special events, yet curiously it does not flourish with pavement cafés and definitely plays second fiddle to Prešernov trg. Its highlights include the views back towards the castle and the flurry of impressive buildings that crowd all around it including the university headquarters, the **Slovenska Filharmonija** (Slovene Philharmonic Hall), the **Uršulinska Cerkev Sv Trojice** (Ursuline Church of the Holy Trinity – *see Churches and cathedrals*) and the **Kazina** – a stunning classical construction. In the centre are a crisscross network of paths, which form a star shape, and myriad benches that make a good venue for enjoying a slice of pizza from the Ljubljanksi Dvor take-away on the square's east side.

**Univerza v Ljubljani** (University of Ljubljana) [3 C5] **C**
Josip Hudetz's epic neo-Renaissance building dominates the southern corner of Kongresni trg. Complete with attractive baroque towers this impressive mansion

was built shortly after the devastating 1895 earthquake. Note the 15 gilded coats of arms, which represent the Carniolan state and Carniolan towns. The fountain in the front courtyard is called Europa and was commissioned to commemorate the EU's recognition of an independent Republic of Slovenia in 1992. A major refurbishment should be completed by summer 2005.

**Slovenska Filharmonija** (Slovene Philharmonic Hall) [3 C5] **C**
Slovenia proudly boasts one of the oldest philharmonic orchestras in the world, established in 1701 as the Academia Philharmonicorum Labacensium and becoming the Philharmonic Society in 1794. Today's hall is the building's third incarnation, as it was destroyed first by fire in 1887 and then the earthquake in 1895. This impressive structure is very different to the wooden construction that originally stood on the spot. Be sure to look at the wavelike shape of the rear of the hall, which backs onto the Ljubljanica. Stunning as it is from the outside the best way to really enjoy the Slovene Philharmonic Hall is to catch a performance by Slovenia's Philharmonic Orchestra or the Chamber Choir who are based in the same building (see *Theatre*).

**Trg Republike** (Republic Square) [3 B5] **C**
Ljubljana's biggest square, the centre of socialist-era Slovenia, is dominated by two hulking towers and the Cankarjev Dom Cultural and Congress Centre (see *Theatre*), all imposing leftovers from the 1980s. The reliefs on the façade of the

Slovenian **Državni Zabor** (National Assembly) on the north side of the square are worth looking at. Sculpted by Zdenko Kalin and Karel Putrih they depict heroic socialist scenes. You can also seek out the small memorial in the adjacent park, the work of Edo Mihevc and Boris Kalin, a tribute to Slovenia's national heroes.

**Slovensko Narodno Gledališče Drama** (Slovene National Drama Theatre) [3 C5] **C**

Designed by Alexander Graf and completed in 1911, the Slovene National Theatre took two years to construct and has an impressive façade. As you pass pop into the entrance hall where you will find the busts of four of the country's most famous classical actors – Počkaj, Linhart, Levstik and Župančič (see *Theatre*).

**Narodna in Univerzitena Knjižnica (NUK)** (National and University Library) [3 C6] **C**

Jože Plečnik was the man behind this deeply impressive library, widely regarded to be his finest work. The futuristic and textured red-brick and stone exterior is constructed entirely from local materials; even the beautifully sculpted doors are striking, but it is the interior that really stands out. Visitors are allowed to climb the grand and austere black marble staircase, flanked by 32 dark marble columns, which leads to the reading room. Unless you are a member or prospective member this is as far as your exploration can go. Much of the lighting, layout and many of the fixtures and fittings inside also originate from Plečnik's studio. The library was built on the site of an old palace that was destroyed in the 1895 earthquake, taking five years to reach completion in 1940 as war broke out across Europe. Local legend has it that Slovene-language literature was secretly tucked away in the depths of the library when the city was occupied from 1941 to 1945.

**Slovenska Akademija Znanosti in Umetnosti** (Slovene Academy of Arts and Sciences) Novi trg 3; tel: 425 6068 [1 D6] **C**
The Lontovž Palace – a stunning baroque mansion has been the institution's nerve centre for almost 70 years and is of major cultural significance to the *Ljubljančani*. For visitors the building's ornate façade, which was designed by Jožef Schemerl and completed between 1786 and 1790, the busts of the academy's former presidents in the entrance hall and Neptune's Fountain – located in the courtyard – are all of interest. Looking across Novi trg to number 5 you will find another of the academy's imposing properties, complete with heavy wooden doors and elaborate decoration below the windows.

**Trg Francoske Revolucije** (French Revolution Square) [1 D6] C
This square is home to the only statue of Napoleon outside of France, known as the Illyrian Monument. It was yet another work of Jože Plečnik, though perhaps not one of his finest with a rather frightening garland-shrouded bust of France's finest perched precariously above the square. Zdenko Kalin's outsized bust of Simon Gregorčič also stands in the square as a memorial to the Slovene poet.

**Križanke** Trg Francoske Revolucije 1; tel: 252 6544 [1 D6] **C**
This former monastic complex, which dates back to the 13th century, was transformed by Jože Plečnik in the 1950s. Today it is regarded as one of the city's premier performance venues (see *Theatre*). Even when there is no show on it is possible to visit the modest Church of St Mary and the baroque Knights Hall, or admire the ornate arcades, busts and sculptures in the grounds; you will find an incarnation of Plečnik himself in the atrium. During the warmer months the Križanke courtyard is a great place to enjoy a coffee from the theatre's small café.

**Krakovo and Trnovo**

Just a short stroll south along the left bank of the Ljubljanica will take you to the twin suburbs of Krakovo and Trnovo, commonly regarded as the oldest and most historic part of the city.

Krakovo is notable for its compact medieval housing, the produce grown in its allotments or market gardens, which is sold at the daily market on Vodnikov trg, and the visible remains of the city's Roman era. On Mirje you find the city's best-preserved stretch of **Rimski zid** (Roman wall), complete with Plečnik modifications. According to locals the Emperor Augustus laid the first stone of the wall in AD14. The slightly incongruous pyramid at the eastern end of the wall stands 6m tall and shows you the minimum height that the Roman wall would have been originally. Other remnants of Emona include an open-air archaeological museum where you can see the ruins of an old Roman house, at Mirje 4. The building's second claim to fame arises from the fact that it was once the home of the Slovene painter Jakopič.

The lively suburb of Trnovo, separated from Krakovo by the Gradaščica Canal, boasts a string of waterfront bars, cafés and restaurants on Eipprova ulica, as well as the **Cerkev Sv Janeza Krstnika** (Church of St John the Baptist – see *Churches and cathedrals*) and the former home of Jože Plečnik, at Karunova 4. Today the architect's house forms part of the **Arhitekturni Muzej** (Architectural Museum – see *Museums*). Plečnik invested a lot of time and energy in landscaping his beloved Trnovo and Krakovo; his influence can be seen today in the form of the gentle sloping embankment of the canal, tree-lined promenades, the **Trnovski Pristan** (Trnovo Pier) and the **Trnovski Most** (Trnovo Bridge) which traverses the Gradaščica. The latter is made with iron and concrete and incorporates four distinctive pyramids in each corner and an obelisk.

**Slovensko Narodno Gledališče Opera in Balet** (SNG Opera) (Slovenian National Opera and Ballet Theatre) [1 B4] **C**

One of Ljubljana's most attractive buildings sits proudly in the centre of a square brimming with impressive architecture. The ornate neo-Renaissance design was the brainchild of Czech architects Hráský and Hrubý, and came into being in 1882. The ornate figures that shelter in niches and adorn the tympanum above the main entrance are the work of sculptor Alojz Grand (see *Theatre*).

**Žale** [off map] **OCC**

B2 *direction Zelena jama.*

Ljubljana's main burial place takes its name from the old Slavic word for cemetery. Opened in 1906 Žale, which is still used today, is laced with grand architecture and layers of history. Graves include those of Italian and Slovene soldiers killed in World War I. The tombs and headstones of Slovenia's famous personalities are intricate works by some of the country's most reputable artists. Legendary Slovenian architect, Jože Plečnik, has also stamped his distinctive mark on the cemetery, including its dramatic colonnaded entrance (1938–40), the Farewell Park, a small chapel and the Tomb of Blumauer (1942). Other notable features include Zdenko Kalin's Fountain of Life, a hexagonal pond flanked by six frolicking figures, Kralj's Tomb of the Menardi Family (1930), Dolina's tombstone of J E Krek (1920), an ossuary containing the bones of Slovenian soldiers who died in World War I and, in the new part of the cemetery, a memorial commemorating the victims of the ten-day war for independence in 1991.

## CHURCHES AND CATHEDRALS

**Stolna Cerkev Sv Nikolaja** (Cathedral of St Nicholas) Dolničarjeva 1; tel: 234 2690 [3 D5:E5] **OT**

Open daily 06.00–12.00 and 15.00–18.00.

The dedication to the patron saint of fishermen and boatmen is fitting for this cathedral located near the Ljubljanica. The original probably stood on the site as far back as the 13th century, but most of today's incarnation is the result of work carried out at the beginning of the 18th century, with the main architect Andrea Pozzo, from Rome, completing work on the city's most important spiritual building in 1706. The cupola was added by Gregor Maček, who took over the construction of the cathedral in the later years. St Nicholas's Cathedral has two entrances and it is worth exploring both. The weighty bronze portal on the south side of the church is known locally as the City Door and is composed of the busts of various bishops of the city, the work of local sculptor Mirsad Begič. Another local artist, Tone Demšar, added an impressive relief to the main, or Slovenian, door in preparation for the Pope's triumphal 1996 visit. The image that now adorns this western portal depicts 1,250 years of Christianity.

Equally noteworthy are the frescos that adorn both the exterior and the interior. On the southern façade you can see Giulio Quaglio's depiction of Mary's annunciation, while his image of Jesus Christ in Jordan adorns the northern wall. Quaglio was also the master behind the ceiling frescos in the nave, which are currently being renovated, with work scheduled to continue until 2006. Janez Wolf's painting of the *Angel's Proclamation of Zahriah Wolf* on the cathedral's eastern façade, Langus's altar painting, Plečnik's bishop's throne and Robba's cherubs, which adorn the altar of Corpus Christi, are also worth seeking out.



**Frančiškanska Cerkev Marijinega Oznanjenja** (Franciscan Church of the Annunciation) Prešernov trg; tel: 425 3001 [1 D4] **C**

One of the symbols of the city, Franciscan monks constructed this attractive pink- coloured church in the middle of the 17th century. Numerous renovations have seen the building alter considerably over time and today's church dates largely from the 18th century. The inspiration for the structure's attractive façade came from a late-Renaissance church in Florence, Santa Maria Novella. Internally, the oldest building on the square, due to its survival of the 1895 earthquake, is less impressive with the most distinguished feature being an altar designed by Francesco Robba. Also look out for Matevž Langus's frescos near the windows, and those added to the nave by Matej Sternen in 1935–36. The adjoining monastery didn't fare so well in the earthquake, with the majority of it needing to be rebuilt. Today it boasts a library housing more than 10,000 books and manuscripts.

**Cerkev Sv Janeza Krstnika** (Church of St John the Baptist) Kolezijska 1; tel: 283 5060 [3 C8] **KT**
Fabled as the place where the romantic Slovene poet, France Prešeren, first spotted Julija Primic – Prešeren's great, if unrequited, love – the church is usually more simply referred to as the Trnovo Church. The original construction dates from the middle of the 18th century. An 1855 reconstruction gave the church a neo-historical appearance, which it kept for four decades. The church's current neo-Romanesque appearance comes from the early 20th century, after the 1895 earthquake took its toll on the church. Metzinger's baroque masterpiece, a stunning altar painting of the church's patron, St John the Baptist, is exquisite. Also look out for frescos by Sternen, and Goršič's mid 19th-century organ.

**Cerkev Sv Florijana** (Church of St Florian) Gornji trg 18; tel: 252 1727 [3 E7] **OT**
This Old Town church was built in 1672 after a devastating fire engulfed this part of the city. The 17th-century locals hoped that by dedicating the church to the patron saint of fires, St Florian, it would be protected against future blazes. Plečnik stamped his indelible mark on the church in the 1930s when he moved the main portal, bricking up the original and placing Robba's statue of St John Nepomuk in front of it. Another of Robba's works, a dramatic depiction of St John being tossed into Prague's Vlatva River from the Czech capital's Charles Bridge, can also be found inside. The church is at its most atmospheric during services and the regular classical concerts.

**Cerkev Sv Jakob** (Church of St James) Levstikov trg; tel: 252 1727 [3 D6:D7] **OT**
Built by Jesuits in 1613 to complement their monastery, this imposing Old Town church boasts the highest belltower in the city, an attractive baroque interior and a Jesuit chapel with intricate stuccowork and an unusual octagonal shape. Before the 1895 earthquake the church actually had two belltowers. The sacristy was also added after the earthquake. Francesco Robba, who lived on Levstikov Square, designed the church's high altar, which was added in 1732. When Plečnik was commissioned to redesign the square in 1933–34 some say he planted a row of poplar trees to hide the church's façade, which he disliked intensely.

**Uršulinska Cerkev Sv Trojice** (Ursuline Church of the Holy Trinity) Slovenska 21; tel: 252 4862 [3 C5] **C**

Located on the western side of regal Kongresni trg, this centrally located church boasts an attractive baroque façade and conceals an enormous multicoloured altar constructed with African marble and altar paintings by Valentin Metzinger. Built in 1726 in Venetian style the church's most striking external features are the six columns that flank its entrance and a balustrade staircase designed by Jože Plečnik.

A copy of the column of the Holy Trinity stands outside. The original column, which is widely believed to be the work of Mislej and Robba and was erected back in 1693 as the *Ljubljančani* gave thanks for those who survived the plague, is in the safe hands of the City Museum.

**Cerkev Šempetrska** (Church of St Peter) Trubarajeva 80 [2 G4] **OCC**
Designed by Italian artist Giovanni Fusconi, the church was constructed between 1729 and 1733. Its somewhat bland exterior is brightened up by Ivan and Helen Vurnik's (of Co-operative Bank fame) attractive mosaics. The depiction of St Peter sits proudly above the main entrance. The interior is also adorned with stunning frescos painted by Franc Jelovšek, a local Slovene artist.

**Srbska Pravoslavna Cerkev** (Serbian Orthodox Church) Prešernova [1 B4] **C**
Partially hidden behind trees the church has an attractive façade and a brightly decorated Orthodox interior. With Primož Trubar standing outside this is a place for one of Ljubljana's other faiths, Orthodox Christians, in a country dominated by Roman Catholicism.

**Cerkev Sv Frančiška Asiškega** (Church of St Francis of Assisi) Černetova 20 [off map] **OCC**
*B22 direction Kamna Gorica to Drenikova stop*
One of Ljubljana's most striking pieces of Plečnik architecture, and the city's most remarkable church, can be found in the suburb of Šišak. A square ground plan and 20 magnificent internal pillars formed the basis of Plečnik's contemporary design, to which a futuristic round belltower was added. Internally the church takes the shape of a covered square complete with colonnades, a flat wooden ceiling and highly individual altars and furnishings.

**Cerkev Sv Mihaela** (Church of St Michael) Barje [off map] **OCC**
*B19 direction Barje*
Another of Plečnik's creations, the Church of St Michael at the heart of the Ljubljana Marshes (Ljubljanske Barje) was built in the periods 1920–28 and 1937–40 around ten pillars. This fortress-like wooden church was constructed on a very tight budget, and innovative ways of cutting the cost reputedly included using sewage pipes rather than concrete for the pillars.

## PARKS AND ESCAPES

**Krajinski Park Tivoli** [1 A1:A4] **TK**
The southeastern fringe of Ljubljana's green lung boasts an immaculately landscaped park that clings tantalisingly on the edge of the city centre. Its walkways, trees,

fountains and benches are the perfect venue for relaxing away from what big-city bustle Ljubljana can muster. The lower level of the park also boasts a children's playground, cafés, fountains and a recreation centre with a pool, roller-skating, tennis and bowling. There is a large glass greenhouse near the park's southern entrance.

**The Krajinski Park Tivoli hills** [off map] **TK**
Tivolski Vrh, Šišenski, Debeli and Rožnik hills, as well as Rkovnik and Mostec collectively make up the largest part of Ljubljana's green lung. The most visited area is Rožnik hill where visitors find the charming Church of St Mary, the Ivan Cankar Memorial Room, and restaurants that feel more like countryside inns. Myriad walking, running and, for the more experienced cyclist, mountain-biking trails weave their way through the densely forested Krajinski. Maps and waymarkers help keep walkers on the right track, although vandals have damaged some of the signposts. If you are feeling really energetic then you can flex your muscles and test your aerobic stamina on a variety of fitness tracks that offer al fresco circuit training.

**Živalski Vrt** (Ljubljana Zoo) Večna pot 70; tel: 244 2188; email: info@zoo-ljubljana.si; www.zoo-ljubljana.si [off map] **TK**
Open daily 09.00–19.00 Apr–Sep; 09.00–18.00 Mar and Oct; and daily 09.00–17.00 Nov–Feb. Admission 800SIT.
The city's zoo has an agreeable forest location, and is home to over 500 animal species. Younger visitors coo over the farm animals, beavers, deer and mouflon

sheep, while older visitors are more appreciative of the zoo's Siberian tiger, giraffes, zebras and leopards. A café, hands-on activities, children's playground and archaeological collection help keep everyone happy.

**Ljubljansko Barje** (Ljubljana Marshes) [off map] **OCC**
B19 *direction Barje*
This peaty marshland 3km from the centre is a real throwback to when marsh dwellers lived in houses built on stilts back in 2000BC. Today the houses have gone, but this boggy land, which is believed to be around two million years old, is still home to around 70 animal species and is visited by more than 250 species of bird each year, making it something of an ornithologist's paradise. Plečnik's **Cerkev Sv Mihaela** (Church of St Michael – see *Churches and cathedrals*) is also here. It is also possible to take a hot-air balloon trip over the marshes (see *Local tour operators*).

**Šmarna Gora** [off map] **OCC**
B8 *direction Brod*
There is no doubting the city's most popular hill. Šmarna Gora, 10km northwest of the city centre, is awash with *Ljubljančani* fleeing the city at weekends. Once a fortress against the Ottomans, today the 669m-high hill is invaded by day trippers seeking a bit of exercise and sweeping views back towards the city. For any reasonably fit adult the trip to the top can be tackled in under an hour. Look out also for the Church of the Holy Mother, with its frescos by Matevž Langus.

# 11 Beyond the City

The local saying goes that 'Ljubljana is just a house and Slovenia but a village', which neatly sums up how compact and easy to get around the country is. In half an hour you can be in the voluminous mountains to the north and west, or if you are in search of the Adriatic Sea the Venetian towns on the coastline are just over an hour's drive to the south down the new highway. Renting your own car is the best plan to open up the country and Avis (see *Local Transport* chapter) have hire offices conveniently located at the airport and at the Hotel Lev, which sits on the main junction for routes leaving the city. Otherwise the bus network is more comprehensive and regular than the train system and serves all main cities and towns from the capital daily. Rail is a fun way to get around if you have time as there are some impressively scenic lines, especially between Bled and Nova Gorica, a line served by the *Old Timer* steam train in the summer months. Even if you are only in the city for a long weekend Slovenia is such a scenically stunning country that you should head out into the surrounding landscapes if you can. The Slovenian Tourist Board website has information about the areas outlined below at www.slovenia-tourism.si. For more detailed information check out *Slovenia: The Bradt Travel Guide* (see *Further Information* chapter, page 228).

## BLED

There are regular and direct bus services from Ljubljana to Bled. Less-frequent train services from Ljubljana stop at Lesce-Bled, from where you have to take a bus or taxi.

This 14,000-year-old alpine lake is simply stunning, a glacial lake fringed by pine trees and vaulting peaks all around. In its heart is an island topped off with a picturesque church. Above, Bled Castle hangs omnipresent over this remarkable natural amphitheatre. It may bustle with tourists for much of the year and there are some unsightly developments dotted around the lake's banks, but on a serene morning when the mists clear and the alpine peaks reflect across the water it is hard not to be spellbound by Bled.

**Bled Tourist Office** Svobode 10; tel: 04 574 1122; www.bled.si
Open Mon–Sat 08.00–21.00, Sun 10.00–21.00 Jul–Aug; Mon–Sat 08.00–19.00, Sun 11.00–18.00 Jun and Sep; Mon–Sat 09.00–19.00, Sun 11.00–16.00 Mar–May and Oct; Mon–Sat 09.00–17.00, Sun 12.00–16.00 Nov–Feb.

## Lake Bled

Walking around the lake takes under two hours and is a great way to really appreciate it. The trail is very easy to follow and a good place to set off is from the Grand Hotel Toplice, if only because you can then finish there and reward yourself with a *kremna rezina* cream cake – a Bled speciality – as you admire the lake from the grand café at the hotel. If your muscles are aching then you can always treat yourself to a massage at the spa in the basement of the hotel. For the less mobile a tourist train skirts the lake during the summer season (550SIT, children 350SIT). For a wonderfully cheesy/romantic experience buy a rose and take your beloved on a horse-drawn carriage – the kiosk just by the Festivalna Dvorna (Festival Hall) charges upwards of 4,000SIT for the ride.

It is also easy to actually get out on to the water. You can rent your own rowing boat and meander around, though the trawl out to the island church from the town end of the lake is far longer than it looks. In summer the water temperature gets up to around 24°C so swimming is also possible – a sublime experience given the views all round. The café at the exclusive Vila Bled – once a palatial home of Tito's – is a good place to relax by the lake away from the crowds.

**Bled Castle** Grajska 25; tel; 04 574 1230
Open daily 08.00–20.00 May–Oct and 08.00–17.00 Nov–Apr. Admission 800SIT, children 500SIT.
Rising improbably over 100m above Lake Bled is the town's striking castle. There have been fortifications on the site since the Middle Ages, but most of the present-day incarnation dates from the 16th century. This was once the seat of power of the legendary Bishops of Brixen and they chose well with a location that affords sweeping views out across the lake and the sweep of Julian Alps that curl all around.

While on a clear day the ramparts with their views and the outdoor café tempt, a visit inside is also compelling. A lot of thought has gone into a recent refurbishment, which has opened up the exhibits in a far more accessible way in the baroque part of the castle next to the 16th-century chapel. On display are period artefacts from the 1700s through to the 1900s, many of them weapons.

**Cerkev Sv Marija Božja** (Church of the Assumption)
Open daily 08.00–sunset.
This picture-postcard-perfect church enjoys the unique setting of its own island right in the heart of Lake Bled. It is an iconic image of Slovenia that adorns a million postcards and countless books and flyers and the hype is justified, as on a misty morning as it looms out of water or at sunset it really is spectacular. Regular gondolas travel out to the island from Bled and also from Mlino (around the lake towards Vila Bled) with return trips costing 1,800SIT. Rowing boats can also be taken out, though swimming is not advised due to the heavy volume of tourist traffic.

## ŠKOFJA LOKA

Škofja Loka is served by very frequent buses and trains from Ljubljana, although the train station is quite a walk from the town's historic core.

On a balmy summer night with the Loka Castle twinkling floodlit above and the old town rambling down the hillside below Škofja Loka takes on an ethereal beauty that Disney can only dream of. The town may be blighted by a handful of apartment blocks on its outskirts and a faceless new town, but the surrounding countryside offers plenty of hiking and cycling opportunities, as well as a brace of remarkable churches at Crngrob and Suha. Much of the protected old town may need more than a lick of paint, but the local authorities have invested in English-language information plaques on buildings and made a real effort in recently revamping the castle's museum. The most interesting streets are the rectangular 'squares' of Mestni trg, Cankarjev trg and Spodnji trg.

**Škofja Loka Tourist Office** Mestni trg 7; tel: 04 512 0268
Open Mon–Fri 08.30-19.00, Sat–Sun 08.30–12.30 and 17.00–19.30 May–Sep; Mon–Fri 08.30–19.00, Sat 08.30–12.30 Oct–Apr.

**Škofja Loka Castle** Grajska pot 13; tel: 04 517 0400
Open Tue–Sun 09.00–18.00 Apr–Sep; Sat–Sun 09.00–17.00 Nov–Mar. Admission 500SIT.
Follow the path that runs up the hill adjacent to the town's medieval walls. In the castle's courtyard you will notice the coats of arms adorning the walls, all of which feature a black king. Local legend puts this down to the days when the black servant of a wealthy landlord saved him from a bear and the king promised that his heroic deed would be remembered forever. A lot of effort has gone into the renovation of the Castle Museum and now there is an English-language guide leaflet as well as information notes by many of the exhibits. Some of the more interesting exhibits are a scale model of the castle showing the original 25m-high central tower, a relief map of the town and a slightly fusty, but nonetheless interesting, natural history section with wildlife from the surrounding countryside. The only real bugbear is that one of the most compelling sections, about the German occupation of the region and subsequent partisan resistance, is only in Slovene though many of the graphic photographs speak for themselves.

**Nacetova Hiša** (Nace's House) Pruštal 74; tel: 04 029 5916
Open by appointment. Admission 400SIT.
This intriguing stone and timber house, which once served as an inn, offers a real insight into local living down the ages, through both its original 16th-century elements and sections that were added in the 18th century. Highlights include the 'black kitchen', a workshop brimming with old tools and a room where 'angry or drunk guests were locked away until they calmed down'. Call ahead and the granddaughter of the last resident who lived here until 1977, opera singer Polde Polenec, may even show you around herself. From the expansive garden there are good views back across the river towards the castle and old town so bring your camera. The tourist office can help you arrange a visit.

## KRANJ

Regular buses and trains from Ljubljana serve Kranj daily. Beware of dodgy characters hanging around both.
Slovenia's raffish fourth-largest city may be blighted by a swathe of factories on its outskirts, but its ethnically diverse citizens – thanks to the workers brought in from other parts of Yugoslavia in the 1970s and 1980s – are justifiably proud of a charming old town that rests spectacularly on a rocky bluff surrounded by the Sava and Kokra rivers, with the lofty peaks of the Kamniške Savinje Alps framing the background. With a sprinkling of accommodation options, numerous bars and a choice of restaurants Kranj invites an overnight stay and is a good base for

exploring the rest of this part of Gorenjska. Kranj is an essential stop for devotees of France Prešeren as he lived here for the final years of his life and died in the old town in a house that is now a museum dedicated to the great Slovene writer.

**Kranj Tourist Office** Koroška cesta 29; tel 04 236 3030
Open Mon–Fri 08.00–19.00, Sat 08.00–12.00.

**France Prešeren's House** Prešernov 7; tel: 04 201 3950
Open Tue–Fri 10.00–12.00 and 17.00–19.00, Sat and Sun 10.00–12.00 and 16.00–18.00 May–Sep; Tue–Fri 10.00–12.00 and 16.00–18.00, Sat and Sun 10.00–12.00 Oct–Apr. Admission 500SIT.
In 2002 the museum reopened after a much-needed revamp and now it has English-language information boards to help guide visitors through. The ground level and the late-Gothic cellar are given over to temporary exhibitions by innovative domestic artists. The museum itself is on the first floor and spreads through the various rooms occupied by the poet during his tenure here from late 1846 to February 1849, when he served as the city's first independent lawyer.

The museum's text – displayed on boards that are not attached to the walls due to a preservation order that bans any changes to the house – cover his whole life, from his school years through to his death and also, of course, his infatuation with Julija Primic, with slightly unnerving sounds of hollering and coughing to add atmosphere. Exhibits include his bed, desk, diaries and even the original entry of his birth in the city's register. The museum staff hope to open up the attic as an extra display area, but they say their hands are currently tied by a legal wrangle over rights to use what is currently a defunct space.

**Town Hall** Glavni trg 4; tel: 04 201 3950
Open Tue–Fri 10.00–12.00 and 17.00–19.00, Sat and Sun 10.00–12.00 and 16.00–18.00 May–Sep; Tue–Fri 10.00–12.00 and 16.00–18.00, Sat and Sun 10.00–12.00 Oct–Apr. Admission 500SIT.
The standout on Glavni trg, with its jumble of Gothic and Renaissance buildings, is perhaps the town hall, which, like Prešeren's House, was originally two buildings and now boasts twin functions as a civic space for weddings and events and also as the Gorenjska Museum. There are two floors of exhibition space with rather dated displays on the evolution of man in the Kranj area, though it does have some interesting artefacts, as well as an exhibit on iron production in the region. The small civic room that is used for weddings has an ornate baroque wooden ceiling and two Renaissance porches. Look out for the early Slavic graves that are visible through transparent panels in the floor of the vestibule – they date back to the 9th century.

**Cerkev Sv Kancijan** (Church of St Cantianus) Glavni trg
The first church on the site dates back to the 6th century, but today's incarnation is based upon a Gothic model that has been added to down the centuries. The central design with its nave and aisles of equal height was taken up as a template in

Cerknica, Radovljica and Škofja Loka. Also look out for the 15th-century frescos depicting angelic musicians and the organ, whose chest dates back to the mid-19th century, but which was refurbished in 2002. If your visit to the town hall has not satiated your interest in Slavic bones then below the northern flank of the church is an ossuary. It is officially closed, but if you ask nicely at the town hall or tourist office they may be able to arrange a visit. Plans have been mooted to reopen the small ossuary with a more modern display set-up, but nothing definite has been agreed.

## POSTOJNA CAVES

Buses leaving for Slovenia's Adriatic coast stop at Postojna and leave Ljubljana bus station at intervals of around 30 minutes. The town is also on the main railway line between the Slovenian capital and Trieste. From Postojna's bus and railway stations the caves are a short taxi or local bus journey away. Postojna is connected to Ljubljana by motorway so it is easy to speed down south and take a guided tour.

The most tourist-friendly cave complex in Slovenia also happens to be one of the most spectacular in the world. The operation is fairly slick with cute little trains rumbling visitors through the myriad stalagmites and stalactites, through you do get the chance to walk amongst the great caverns and bizarre formations. The only way to see the caves unless you are on a scientific research trip is to go on the 1¼-hour guided tour.

The tour starts with a stampede towards the entrance where the cute toytown trains await. Do not be fooled by their innocuous appearance, though, as they rattle off downhill for 2km at a fair rate and if you pop your head out for a closer look at the stalactites you are liable to lose it. The line (laid as far back as 1872) skirts myriad stalactites and stalagmites on a narrow route in. On arrival the hordes are divided up by language and trooped off for a 1½km walk, starting with a stroll up the Great Mountain and then a wander through the galleries and caverns that house myriad sizes and shapes of stalactites, stalagmites and pillars with nicknames such as 'spaghetti'. The trail then drops down to the sturdy Russian Bridge, built by POWs in World War I that leads through to the aptly named Beautiful Cave before entering the Winter Hall where the Brilliant and Diamond formations have become the rather phallic symbols of the caves. The walking section ends in the Grand Hall, a voluminous space that is used for concerts, though its impressive 30m rock ceiling is somewhat tainted by a tacky souvenir stand that is meant to separate you from your tolars while you wait for the trains out.

**Postojna Tourist Information** Jamska 30; tel: 05 700 0100; www.postojna-cave.com

## ALSO WORTH A VISIT

**Lake Bohinj** Much larger and less touristy than Bled, this is a good choice if you are looking for a quieter and more relaxed experience. The walk around the lake takes around five–six hours and offers a real break away from it all, perfect if you are on a long weekend trying to escape the stress of a hectic home life.
Tourist office tel: 04 574 6010; www.bohinj.si.

**Kamnik** Just a half-hour drive north of Ljubljana is the pretty little town of Kamnik, perfect for a minimum-effort day trip. The spectacular Kamniške Savinje Alps loom behind the compact old centre. There is not too much to do bar float around the sprinkling of cafés, bars and churches and admire the view.
Tourist office tel: 01 839 1470; www.turizem.kamnik.si.

**Kranjska Gora** One of the country's main ski resorts enjoys a spectacular setting in the Julian Alps. It may be a bit tacky and brash, but it has all the facilities for a one- or two-night ski break during the season. At other times it is worth visiting for a spot of hiking or serious climbing in the Julian Alps, which strike out dramatically above.
Tourist office tel: 04 588 5020; www.kranjska-gora.si.

**Piran** One of the most remarkable Venetian-era towns on the Adriatic coastline. It is an effort to get down south to Piran and the traffic can be a nightmare on busy summer weekends when the whole of Ljubljana seems to be heading to the same place, but Piran is worth it. A vaulting Venetian belltower – styled on the *campanile* in Venice – overlooks the rocky promontory which the orange roof-tiled town houses spill down towards Piran's dramatic dalliance with the sea.
Tourist office tel: 05 673 0220; www.portoroz.si.

**Škojcan Caves** This UNESCO World Heritage-listed cave complex may not be as renowned worldwide as Postojna, but if anything they are more spectacular and

certainly less blighted by tourist development. Well worth the slightly longer journey.
Ticket office tel: 05 763 2840.

**Vipava Valley** Wine connoisseurs whose interest in Slovenian wine has been stimulated in the city can drive south down the motorway to the Vipava Valley. This green oasis is set spectacularly on the cusp of the rugged Karst region and abounds with cute villages and sweeping vineyards. There are numerous small-scale producers and a dedicated wine road has now been opened. Pop into the Slovenian TIC in Ljubljana who may have a copy of the map or the local tourist information in the town of Adjovščina. When visiting the vineyards calling ahead is a good idea with Tilia a typically rewarding cellar to visit. We idled away a day with the enthusiastic owner sampling his produce and, of course, walking away with a hefty clump of his wines.
Tilia tel: 05 364 6683; email: tilia@lemut.net. Adjovščina tourist office tel: 05 366 3900.

# Language

The official language of the Republic of Slovenia is Slovene, a Slavic language that has a lot in common with the languages spoken by Slovenia's Croatian, Serbian, Bosnian and Montenegrin neighbours. Slovene uses a version of the Roman alphabet with 25 letters: *a b c č d e f g h I j k I m n o p r s š t u v z ž*. Many letters are pronounced as they are in English, but there are a number of key exceptions.

## PRONUNCIATION

### Vowels

*a* – short pronunciation like 'a' in 'hat'
*a* – long pronunciation like 'a' in 'rather' (to confuse things it can also sound like the 'u' in 'hut'
e – short pronunciation like the 'e' in 'vet'
e – long pronunciation like the 'ea' in 'wear'
*i* – short pronunciation like the 'i' in 'pink'
*i* – long pronunciation like the 'ee' in 'seem'
*o* – short pronunciation like the 'o' in 'off'
*o* – long pronunciation like the 'aw' in 'paw'
*u* – like the 'oo' in 'foot'

### Consonants

*c* – like the 'ts' in 'rats'
*d* – like the 'd' in 'dog'
*g* – like the 'g' in 'gold'
*j* – like the 'y' in 'yacht'
*l* – like the 'l' in 'leak'
*r* – Slovenes roll the letter 'r', pronouncing it from the tip of their tongue, in the same way as the French and the Scots
*v* – can sound like the 'v' in 'vodka', but more often takes the form of the 'w' in 'water'

### Consonants with carons

*č* – like the 'ch' in 'chomp'
*š* – like the 'sh' in 'sham'
*ž* – like the 'su' in 'treasure'

## USEFUL WORDS AND EXPRESSIONS

### Basics

| | | | |
|---|---|---|---|
| hello | *zdravo* | goodbye | *nasvidenje* |
| good day | *dober dan* | yes | *da/ja* |
| good morning | *dobro jutro* | no | *ne* |
| good evening | *dober večer* | please | *prosim* |

| | | | |
|---|---|---|---|
| here you are | *izvolite* | Mrs | *gospa* |
| thank you (very much) | *hvala (lepa)* | Miss | *gospodična* |
| excuse me | *dovolite mi, prosim* | what? | *kaj?* |
| sorry | *oprostite* | why? | *zakaj?* |
| Mr | *gospod* | when? | *kdaj?* |
| | | who? | *kdo?* |

## Conversation

| | |
|---|---|
| How are you? | *Kako ste?* |
| Very well thank you. | *Zelo dobro hvala.* |
| My name is . . . | *Imenujem se . . .* |
| What's your name? | *Kako vam je ime?* |
| I am English/Scottish/Welsh/Irish/American/Canadian/Australian. | *Sem Anglež/Škot/Valižan/Irec/Američan/Kanadčan/Avstralec.* |
| Where are you from? | *Od kod ste?* |

## Family

| | | | |
|---|---|---|---|
| aunt | *teta* | husband | *mož* |
| brother | *brat* | mother | *mama* |
| daughter | *hči* | sister | *sestra* |
| father | *oče* | son | *sin* |
| grandfather | *stari oče* | uncle | *stric* |
| grandmother | *stara mama* | wife | *žena* |

## Language

| | |
|---|---|
| Do you speak English? | *Ali govorite angleško?* |
| I don't speak Slovene | *Ne govorim slovensko* |
| Please speak more slowly | *Govorite počasneje prosim* |
| I understand | *Razumem* |
| I don't understand | *Ne razumem* |
| Please write it down | *Prosim zapišite.* |
| How do you say . . . ? | *Kako rečete . . . ?* |

## Accommodation

| | |
|---|---|
| inn | *krčma* |
| pension | *prenočišci* |
| guesthouse | *gostišče* |
| campsite | *kamping* |
| youth hostel | *mladinsko prenočišče* |
| student dormitory | *študentski dom* |
| rooms available | *proste sobe* |
| Do you have a single/double room? | *Ali imate prosto enoposteljno/ dvoposteljno sobo?* |
| with a bath/shower | *s kadjo/prho* |
| Could you wake me at . . . ? | *Ali me lahko zbudite ob . . . ?* |
| I'd like a . . . | *Rad bi . . .* (male) *Rada bi . . .* (female) |

| | |
|---|---|
| towel | *brisača* |
| room | *soba* |
| bed | *postelja* |
| dorm bed | *skupna ležišča* |
| How much is it per night/per person? | *Koliko stane na noč/po osebi?* |
| Is breakfast included? | *Ali je zajtrk vključen?* |
| full board | *polni penzion* |
| half board | *polpenzion* |
| Can I see the room? | *Ali lahko vidim sobo?* |
| I have a reservation | *Imam rezervacijo* |

## Health and emergencies

| | | | |
|---|---|---|---|
| police | *policija* | hand | *roka* |
| hospital | *bolnišnica* | blood | *kri* |
| ambulance | *rešilec* | chest | *prsni koš* |
| chemist/pharmacy | *lekarna* | leg/foot | *noga* |
| dentist | *zobozdravnik* | head | *glava* |
| doctor | *doktor* | shoulder | *rama* |
| ache/pain | *bolečina* | stomach | *želodec* |
| arm | *laket* | | |

## Directions

| | | | |
|---|---|---|---|
| Where is the . . . ? | *Kje je . . . ?* | opposite | *nasproti* |
| turn left/right | *obrnite levo/desno* | here/there | *tu/tam* |
| near/far | *blizu/daleč* | north | *sever* |
| go straight ahead | *pojdite naravnost naprej* | south | *jug* |
| | | east | *vzhod* |
| behind | *zadaj* | west | *zahod* |
| in front of | *spredaj* | | |

## Driving/transport

| | | | |
|---|---|---|---|
| airport | *letališče* | garage | *garaža* |
| aeroplane | *letalo* | petrol | *bencin* |
| bus | *avtobus* | petrol station | *bencinska črpalka* |
| train | *vlak* | motorway/highway | *avtocesta* |
| railway station | *železniška postaja* | road | *cesta* |
| platform | *peron* | puncture | *preluknjana zračnica/ avtomobilska guma* |
| bus station | *avtobusna postaja* | | |
| bus stop | *avtobusno postajališče* | | |
| | | map | zemljevid |
| timetable | *vozni red* | bicycle | kolo |
| car | *avto* | ferry | trajekt |

| | |
|---|---|
| A one-way ticket to . . . please | *Enosmerno vozovnico za . . . prosim* |
| A return ticket to . . . please | *Povratno vozovnico za . . . prosim* |
| Can I reserve a seat? | *Ali lahko rezerviram sedež?* |
| What time does the bus/train leave? | *Kdaj odpelje avtobus/vlak?* |
| Stop here please | *Ustavite tukaj prosim* |

## Signs

| | | | |
|---|---|---|---|
| entrance/exit | *vhod/izhod* | prohibited | *prepovedano* |
| open/closed | *odprto/zaprto* | (male/female) | *(moško/žensko)* |
| arrivals/departures | *prihod/odhod* | toilets | *stranišče* |
| information | *informacije* | | |

## Places

| | | | |
|---|---|---|---|
| bank | *banka* | church | *cerkev* |
| bay | *morski zaliv* | city | *veliko mesto* |
| beach | *plaža* | fair | *sejem* |
| bridge | *most* | field | *polje* |
| castle | *grad* | forest | *gozd* |
| cathedral | *stolnica* | fountain | *vodnjak* |
| cave | *jama* | garden | *vrt* |
| centre | *središče* | hill | *hrib, grič* |
| chapel | *kapelica* | house | *hiša* |

| | |
|---|---|
| island | *tok* |
| lake | *jezero* |
| laundry | *pralnica* |
| market | *tržnica* |
| monastery | *samostan* |
| mountain | *gora* |
| museum | *muzej* |
| Old Town/City | *stari del mesta* |
| port | *pristanišče* |
| post office | *pošta* |
| river | *reka* |
| school | *šola* |
| sea | *morje* |
| shop | *trgovina* |
| shopping centre | *nakupovalni center* |
| (main) square | *(glavni) trg* |
| street | *ulica* |
| therapeutic spa | *toplice* |
| tower | *stolp* |
| town | *mesto* |
| town hall | *mestna hiša* |
| valley | *dolina* |
| village | *vas* |
| waterfall | *slap* |

## Eating and drinking

| | |
|---|---|
| good appetite | *dober tek* |
| restaurant | *restavracija* |
| taverna | *gostilna* |

## Fish

| | |
|---|---|
| dorada | *orada* |
| fried fish | *ocvrta riba* |
| grilled fish | *riba na žaru* |
| lobster | *jastog* |
| mussels | *školjke* |
| octopus | *hobotnica* |

| | | | |
|---|---|---|---|
| prawns | *rakci* | sole | *morski list* |
| salmon | *losos* | squid | *lignji* |
| seabass | *brancin* | trout | *postrv* |
| shrimps | *škampi* | tuna | *tuna* |

## Meat

| | | | |
|---|---|---|---|
| air-dried ham | *pršut* | mixed grill | *meso na žaru* |
| beef | *govedina* | pork | *svinjina* |
| chicken | *piščanec* | rabbit | *zajec* |
| goulash | *golaž* | sausage | *klobasa* |
| ham | *šunka* | turkey | *puran* |
| horse steak | *zrezek* | veal | *teletina* |
| lamb | *jagnjetina* | venison | *divjačina* |

## Fruit and vegetables

| | | | |
|---|---|---|---|
| apple | *jabolka* | cabbage | *zelje* |
| apricot | *marelica* | carrots | *korenje* |
| artichoke | *artičoke* | cherry | *češnja* |
| asparagus | *beluši* | courgette | *bučke* |
| banana | *banana* | cucumber | *kumara* |
| basil | *bazilika* | garlic | *česen* |
| beans | *fižol* | grape | *grozdje* |

lemon *limona*
melon *melona*
mushrooms *gobe*
(black) olive *(črne) olive*
onions *čebula*
orange *pomaranča*
peach *breskev*
pear *hruška*
peas *grah*
pepper *poper*
pineapple *ananas*
plum *silva*
potato *krompir*
raspberry *malina*
ruccola *rukola*(green/mixed) *(zelena/mešana)*
salad *solata*
spinach *špinača*
strawberry *jagoda*
tomato *paradižnik*
watermelon *lubenica*

## Dessert

ice-cream *sladoled*
strudel *zavitek*
traditional cream cake *krema rezina*
traditional Prekmurje dessert *gibanica*
traditional Slovenian cake *potica*

## Drinks

beer *pivo*
coffee *kava*
milky coffee *bela kava*
espresso with milk *macchiato*

| | | | |
|---|---|---|---|
| fruit juice | *sok* | wine (white, red, rosé) | *vino (belo, črno, roze)* |
| (mineral) water | *(mineralna) voda* | | |
| tea (with milk/ lemon) | *čaj (z mlekom/ z limono)* | | |

## Miscellaneous

| | | | |
|---|---|---|---|
| beef/mushroom/ bean/vegetable/ fish soup | *goveja/fižolova/ gobova/zelenjavna/ ribja juha* | cheese | *sir* |
| | | (sour) cream | *(kisla) smetana* |
| | | egg | *jajce* |
| bread | *kruh* | omelette | *omleta* |

## Meals and useful words

| | | | |
|---|---|---|---|
| baked | *pečen* | glass | *kozarec* |
| boiled | *kuhano* | grilled | *na žaru* |
| bowl | *skleda* | knife | *nož* |
| breakfast | *zajtrk* | lunch | *kosilo* |
| cup | *skodelica* | plate | *plošča* |
| dinner | *večerja* | roast | *pečenka* |
| fork | *vilica* | spoon | *žlica* |
| fried | *ocvrto* | | |

## Other useful words and phrases

| | |
|---|---|
| The bill, please | *Račun prosim* |
| Where is the toilet? | *Kje je stranišče?* |
| What's the time? | *Koliko je ura?* |
| How much does this cost? | *Koliko stane?* |
| maybe | *mogoče* |
| good | *dober* |
| bad | *slab* |
| big | *mala* |
| small | *velika* |
| not much | *komaj da / ne veliko* |
| you're welcome | *prosim / ni za kaj* |
| married | *poročen / poročena* (male / female) |
| money | *denar* |

## Numbers

| | | | |
|---|---|---|---|
| 0 | *nič* | 6 | *šest* |
| 1 | *ena* | 7 | *sedem* |
| 2 | *dve* | 8 | *osem* |
| 3 | *tri* | 9 | *devet* |
| 4 | *štiri* | 10 | *deset* |
| 5 | *pet* | 11 | *enajst* |

| | | | |
|---|---|---|---|
| 12 | *dvanajst* | 30 | *trideset* |
| 13 | *trinajst* | 40 | *štirideset* |
| 14 | *štirinajst* | 50 | *petdeset* |
| 15 | *petnajst* | 60 | *šestdeset* |
| 16 | *šestnajst* | 70 | *sedemdeset* |
| 17 | *sedemnajst* | 80 | *osemdeset* |
| 18 | *osemnajst* | 90 | *devetdeset* |
| 19 | *devetnajst* | 100 | *sto* |
| 20 | *dvajset* | 1,000 | *tisoč* |

## Time, days and months

| | | | |
|---|---|---|---|
| What is the time? | *Koliko je ura?* | Friday | *petek* |
| It is ... | *Ura je ...* | Saturday | *sobota* |
| two o'clock | *dve* | Sunday | *nedelja* |
| nine o'clock | *devet* | day | *dan* |
| eight thirty | *pol devetih* | today | *danes* |
| quarter to five | *četrt na pet* | yesterday | *včeraj* |
| quarter past eleven | *enajst in četrt* | tomorrow | *jutri* |
| Monday | *ponedeljek* | morning | *zjutraj* |
| Tuesday | *torek* | noon | *poldan* |
| Wednesday | *sreda* | afternoon | *popoldne* |
| Thursday | *četrtek* | evening | *večer* |

| | |
|---|---|
| night | *noč* |
| January | *januar* |
| February | *februar* |
| March | *marec* |
| April | *april* |
| May | *maj* |
| June | *junij* |
| July | *julij* |
| August | *avgust* |
| September | *september* |
| October | *oktober* |
| November | *november* |
| December | *december* |

## Colours

| | |
|---|---|
| black | *črno* |
| white | *belo* |
| red | *rdeče* |
| green | *zeleno* |
| blue | *modro* |
| orange | *oranžno* |

13

# Further Information

## MAGAZINES AND NEWSPAPERS

### Entertainment

*Ljubljana Calling* is a monthly listings magazine, which can be hard to find in its printed version but is available at some of the city's hotels.

*Ljubljana Life* is a quarterly magazine with plenty of tourist information and some longer articles and is available at tourist information centres and hotels throughout the city.

### News and current affairs

*Slovenia News* is a weekly colour magazine with features on personalities and cultural events. Look out for copies at TICs, cafés and hotels throughout the city.

*Slovenia Times* is an excellent English-language monthly newspaper that covers politics, the economy and also has occasional tourist supplements; again this can be picked up at TICs and hotels.

## BOOKS

### Architecture

Gooding, Mel and Music, Marko and Fiennes, Mark *National & University Library, Ljubljana, Slovenia, 1936–39, by Jože Plečnik (Architecture in Detail Series)* Phaidon Press, 1997. In-depth examination of what many consider to be Plečnik's finest architectural achievement.

Hrausky, Andrej and Koželj *Architectural Guide to Ljubljana: 100 Selected Buildings* Rokus, 2002. Insightful guide to Ljubljana's impressive architecture. Hard to buy outside Slovenia.

## Fiction

Blatnik, Andrej *Skinswaps (Writing from an Unbound Europe)* Northwestern University Press, 1998. Sixteen short stories by the popular Slovene post-modern writer.

Debeljak, Ales *The City & the Child* White Pine Press, 1999. Anthology of contemporary poems by the popular Slovene poet.

Holton, Milne and Taufer, Veno (Translators) *Waterlings* Northwestern University Press, 2000. Six epic Slovenian poems about mythical water beings translated into English.

Mozetič, Brane *Butterflies* Meeting Eyes Bindery, 2004. Poetry anthology.

## History

Benderley, Jill and Craft, Ivan *Independent Slovenia* Palgrave Macmillan, 1997. In-depth study of Slovenia's political and economic development since 1990.

Benderley, Jill *Independent Slovenia: Origins, Movements, Prospects* Palgrave Macmillan, 1996. Decent introduction to Slovenia and the country's recent political and economic history.

Carmichael, Cathie and Gow, James *Slovenia & the Slovenes* Indiana University Press, 2001. Thorough examination of history, economics, politics and culture in 20th-century Slovenia.

Fink-Hafner, Danica and Robbins, John R *Making a New Nation: Formation of Slovenia* Dartmouth, 1996. Examining the role of Slovenia in the Socialist Federal Republic of Yugoslavia and its emergence as an independent country.

*War in Slovenia: From first 'attacks' on YPA to final victory over the Yugoslav Army* Ljubljana International Press Centre, 1991. Fascinating insight into Slovenia's ten-day war of independence with Serbia. Limited availability.

Mrak, Mojmir and Rojec, Matja and Rojec, Marika (Editors) *Slovenia: From Yugoslavia to the European Union* World Bank, 2004. Weighty but informative read focusing on the reasons for the dissolution of Yugoslavia and Slovenia's political and economic development since 1991, including its integration into the EU.

Prunk, Janko *A Brief History of Slovenia: Historical background of the Republic of Slovenia* Zalozba Mihelac, 1994. Useful introduction to Slovenia and its history. Can be a little too general at times.

## Mountaineering/hiking

Brown, Simon *Walking in the Julian Alps* Cicerone Press, 1993. Now something of a classic, a range of easy-to-follow walks for all levels of fitness and experience.

Mihelič, Tine *Mountaineering in Slovenia: The Julian Alps and Kamnik and Savinja Alps* Cordee, 2003. Comprehensive guide for those interested in tackling Slovenia's mountains.

Newbury *A Guide to Walks & Scrambles in the Julian Alps based on Kranjska Gora* Zlatorog Publications, 2003. Excellent rambling guide with trails suitable for everyone from the novice to the experienced walker.

## Travel

McKelvie, Robin and Jenny *Slovenia: The Bradt Travel Guide* Bradt Travel Guides, 2005

## BOOKSHOPS (see *Shopping*)

**Geonavtik** Kongresni trg 1; tel: 252 7027 [3 C5] **C**

**Knjigarna Novak** Wolfova 8; tel: 422 3410 [3 D5] **C**

**Mladinska Knjiga** Slovenska 29; tel: 241 0651 [3 C5] **C**

**Mladinska Knjiga** Nazorjeva 1; tel: 241 4700 [1 D4] **C**

## MAPS

Geodetski zavod Slovenije dd (www.gzs-dd.si), who produce excellent maps of Ljubljana and Slovenia, kindly gave their permission for us to use one of their city maps as a basis for Bradt's cartographers. Their maps are available in hotels, TICs and bookstores in Slovenia. Bookstores and online retailers outside of Slovenia should also stock maps produced by Geodetski zavod Slovenije dd.

**Kod & Kam** Trg Francoske Revolucije 7; tel: 200 2732 [3 C6] **C**
Stock a wide range of maps and road atlases.

## WEBSITES

### Tourist information

**Ljubljana Tourism** www.ljubljana-tourism.si

**Slovenia Tourism** www.slovenia-tourism.si

**Slovenian Landmarks** www.burger.si

### General information

**State Portal of the Republic of Slovenia** www.e-uprava.gov.si/e-uprava/en/portal.euprava

## Local transport

**Avtobusna Postaja Ljubljana** (Ljubljana Bus Station) www.ap-ljubljana.si

## Daily newspapers

**Delo** www.delo.si

**Dnevnik** www.dnevnik.si

**Večer** www.vecer.si

## Business news

**Slovenia Business Week** www.gzs.si

## English-language news

**Republic of Slovenia Public Relations and Media Office** www.uvi.si/eng

**Slovenian Bulletin** http://geocities.com/ljubljanalife/News.htm

**Slovenia Business Report** www.gvrevija.com

**Slovenija Magazine** www.zdruzenje-sim.si

**Slovenia News** www.uvi.si/eng/slovenia/publications/slovenia-news

**Slovenia Times** www.sloveniatimes.com

## Lifestyle and culture

**Ljubljana Calling** www.ljubljana-calling.com

**Ljubljana Digital Media Lab** www.ljudmila.org

**Ljubljana Life** www.geocities.com/ljubljanalife
**Slovenian Ministry of Culture** www.kultura.gov.si

## Gay Ljubljana

**Ljubljana Digital Media Lab** www.ljudmila.org
**Slovenian Queer Resources Directory** www.ljudmila.org/siqrd

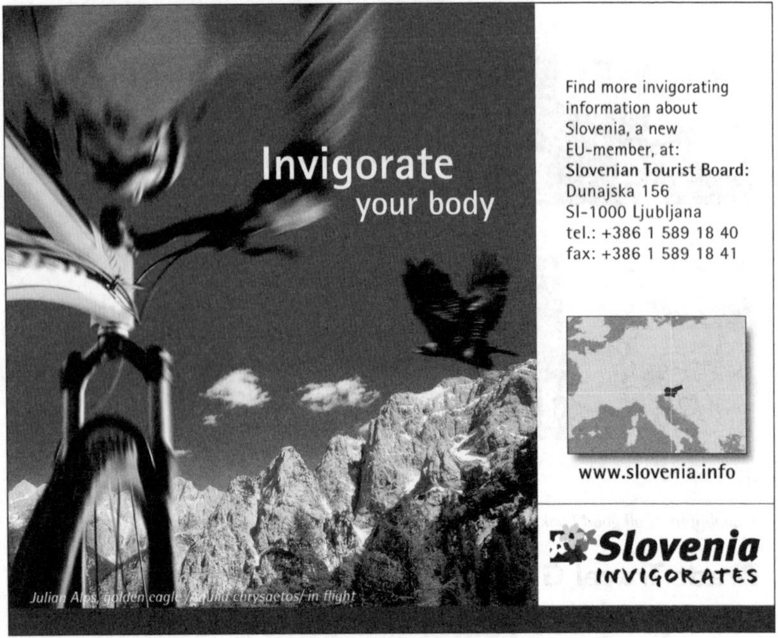
Invigorate
your body
Julian Alps, golden eagle /Aquila chrysaetos/ in flight
Find more invigorating information about Slovenia, a new EU-member, at:
Slovenian Tourist Board:
Dunajska 156
SI-1000 Ljubljana
tel.: +386 1 589 18 40
fax: +386 1 589 18 41
www.slovenia.info
Slovenia
INVIGORATES

# Index

***Page numbers in bold indicate major entries***